French Caribbean Cuisine

THE HIPPOCRENE
COOKBOOK LIBRARY

Africa and Oceania
Best of Regional African Cooking
Traditional South African Cookery
Taste of Eritrea
Good Food from Australia

Asia and Middle East
The Best of Taiwanese Cuisine
Imperial Mongolian Cooking
The Best of Regional Thai Cuisine
Japanese Home Cooking
The Best of Korean Cuisine
Egyptian Cooking
Sephardic Israeli Cuisine
Healthy South Indian Cooking
The Indian Spice Kitchen
The Cuisine of the Caucasus Mountains
Afghan Food and Cookery
The Art of Persian Cooking
The Art of Turkish Cooking
The Art of Uzbek Cooking

Mediterranean
Best of Greek Cuisine, Expanded Edition
Taste of Malta
A Spanish Family Cookbook
Tastes of North Africa

Western Europe
Art of Dutch Cooking, Expanded Edition
A Belgian Cookbook
Cooking in the French Fashion (bilingual)
Cuisines of Portuguese Encounters
The Swiss Cookbook
The Art of Irish Cooking
Feasting Galore Irish-Style
Traditional Food from Scotland
Traditional Food from Wales
The Scottish-Irish Pub and Hearth Cookbook
A Treasury of Italian Cuisine (bilingual)

Scandinavia
Best of Scandinavian Cooking
The Best of Finnish Cooking
The Best of Smorgasbord Cooking
Good Food from Sweden
Tastes & Tales of Norway
Icelandic Food & Cookery

Central Europe
All Along the Rhine
All Along the Danube
Best of Austrian Cuisine
Bavarian Cooking
The Best of Czech Cooking
The Best of Slovak Cooking
The Art of Hungarian Cooking
Hungarian Cookbook
Polish Heritage Cookery
The Best of Polish Cooking
Old Warsaw Cookbook
Old Polish Traditions
Treasury of Polish Cuisine (bilingual)
Poland's Gourmet Cuisine
The Polish Country Kitchen Cookbook

Eastern Europe
Art of Lithuanian Cooking
Best of Albanian Cooking
Traditional Bulgarian Cooking
Best of Croatian Cooking
Taste of Romania
Taste of Latvia
The Best of Russian Cooking
Traditional Russian Cuisine (bilingual)
The Best of Ukrainian Cuisine

Americas
Argentina Cooks
A Taste of Haiti
A Taste of Quebec
Cajun Women Cook
Cooking the Caribbean Way
French Caribbean Cuisine
Mayan Cooking
The Honey Cookbook
The Art of Brazilian Cookery
The Art of South American Cookery
Old Havana Cookbook (bilingual)

French Caribbean Cuisine

Stéphanie Ovide

Preface by
Maryse Condé

Drawings by
Maurita Magner

HIPPOCRENE BOOKS, INC.
NEW YORK

Cover paintings by Didier Spindler.
Drawings by Maurita Magner
Illustrations by Bernard Lamotte / © Vogue, Condé Nast Publications Inc.

Book and jacket design by Acme Klong Design, Inc.

For more information, address;
HIPPOCRENE BOOKS, INC.
171 Madison Avenue
New York, NY 10016

ISBN 0-7818-0925-8
Cataloging-in-Publication Data available from the Library of Congress.
Printed in the United States of America.

To my grandfather, George Emanuel Nicolas

"For we consider cooking one of the fine arts, a minor one per-
haps, but unquestionably one of them. Like painting or music, like
poetry or choreography, isn't the purpose of cooking to beautify
human life?

> Mapie, the Countess de Toulouse-Lautrec
> in *La Cuisine de France*, Bonanza Books, New York.

Acknowledgements

A special thank to my friend and artist Didier Spindler, who painted the cover of this book; Maurita Magner who illustrated the book and whose advice is always precious; and the Condé Nast Archives for allowing me to use illustrations from *Vogue* magazine. I would like to thank the following people without whom I could not have written this book: my husband Marco, who has always been patient and encouraging; my mother Sylvie Nicolas for lending me her kitchen and coming with me on Sundays to the market; my father Jacques Ovide for sharing his memories and recipes; my sister Julie and my brothers Jonathan and Robinson for being my best critics; my aunts Marie-Claude Nicolas and Elizabeth Nicolas and my uncle Alain Nicolas for their love of Creole tradition; Ary and Nicole Vila for sharing with me their delicious recipes; my grandmothers Yvonne Ovide and Louisette Gauduchon for passing on to me the tradition of Caribbean cuisine; my grand aunt Serge for sharing her recipes; Mamie Zea for her delicious cuisine; my godmother Evelyne Caillaud who taught me the refinement of Creole cuisine; the amazing cooks Rita, Sandra, Julie, Lyne, Lisette, Colette, Hoff Fala and Fofo; Jean Paul Colas, chef at L'auberge des Petits Saints; Charles D. Scheips Jr., director of the Condé Nast Archives; Anne-Marie Ovide; Gilles Lefebvre; Catherine Baudinière; Hélène Laboissiere; Claudie and Jacques Lunes; Jean-Pierre Ovide; Marie-Francoise and Dominique Percevault; my dear friends Carole and Florian; Elizabeth Greenberg; Michelle Tolini; Ena and David Wojciechowski; Laurent Guengant; Toni Campione; Fumiko Takahagi; Alexandre Mabillon for being supportive at all times; Nour, Nel and Serge Caillaud; Gregory and Mowgli Laps, Clemence and Julien Ragazzoni, Morgan, Vanille and Canelle Nicolas, Anthony and Arnaud Lunes, Fabrice, Sandrine and Remy Vila; Michael Stier from Condé Nast Publications; and finally a special thank to my publisher George Blagowidow, who trusted me to write this book.

Préface

J'aime à le répéter sans fausse modestie : après une quinzaine d'ouvrages, j'ignore encore si je suis une bonne romancière, alors que sans doute possible, je le sais, je l'affirme, je suis une excellente cuisinière. Depuis des décennies, je régale mon mari, mes enfants, mes hôtes. Un de mes rêves qui—parmi tant d'autres—ne se réalisera jamais, serait de posséder un restaurant dont j'établirais la carte au gré de mes fantaisies, de mes rencontres, de mes découvertes, ici et là au hasard de voyages, ou tout simplement de visites chez des amis et que je façonnerais selon ma propre imagination. Je ne manquerais pas d'y marier table et littérature. Au dessert, on dégusterait des poèmes ; au café, on savourerait des extraits de romans ; après les repas, on échangerait sans pédanterie des appréciations sur la technique romanesque et les diverses stratégies narratives.

Ma mère, qui fille de cuisinière se louant à l'année voyait peut-être les choses sans romantisme, affirmait qu'une femme intelligente n'est capable de préparer aucun plat. Aussi, lors des séjours en France, privée de ses aides restées à la Guadeloupe, elle nourrissait la famille d'oeufs durs, de conserves de petits pois et de sardines à l'huile. Je m'inscris en faux contre cette conception élitiste. Pour moi, cuisiner est un art qui exige autant de créativité et d'audace que celui d'écrire. Comme en littérature, il faut inventer. Il faut défier l'attente du convive/ lecteur en ne craignant jamais d'innover, d'expérimenter au risque de le surprendre, voire de le choquer avant d'emporter son adhésion. Pour moi, l'art de cuisiner peut aussi se comparer à celui de peindre : ajouter à un plat des dés de poivron vert, l'entremêler de grains de maïs doré, l'agrémenter d'une rondelle de piment rouge, safraner du riz dans le but de parfaire une palette de couleurs. Sacrilège ? Je n'ai jamais pu contempler un tableau de Jackson Pollock sans avoir l'eau à la bouche. « Abstract expressionism » dit-on ? Pour moi, pas si abstrait que cela.

Voilà pourquoi je n'ai pas hésité longtemps avant d'accepter de préfacer l'ouvrage de Stéphanie Ovide. Elle me fournissait l'occasion de libérer une part insatisfaite et peu connue de moi-même, cachée sous les romans, les pièces de théâtre, les articles de critiques littéraires et aussi les cours et les conférences.

La cuisine antillaise est une mosaïque. C'est une invitation au voyage puisqu'épousant les méandres d'un peuplement-mosaïque, elle se situe au carrefour de trois traditions. Nourris de « racines », de « pois », de bas morceaux de porc (museaux, oreilles, queues), de morue salée et de hareng saur, les esclaves venus d'Afrique ne se contentèrent pas de remplir des estomacs laissés perpétuellement vides par l'incurie de leurs maîtres, ils posèrent les fondements de l'édifice culinaire. Les Européens et les Indiens venus supplémenter la main d'oeuvre servile après l'abolition de l'esclavage, ajoutèrent leurs couleurs et leurs saveurs empruntées à leurs terres d'origine et firent le reste. Dans la Caraïbe plurielle, la Martinique et la Guadeloupe présentent la particularité d'avoir été—pour le meilleur et pour le pire— colonisées par les Français, c'est à dire par un peuple amoureux à l'excès de la table. La France, on le sait, a pratiquement conféré une dimension religieuse au bien manger. Les chefs sont révérés comme des grands-prêtres. Le Gault et Millau (rien à voir avec la modestie et le souci pratique du Zagat Survey) fait figure de Bible. Traditionnellement arrosé de vins judi- cieusement choisis pour rehausser la variété des goûts, le repas de fête s'é- tale pendant des heures. Et ce n'est pas un hasard si dans ce pays, la lutte contre « la mal-bouffe », symbolisée par les Mac Do et autres fast-foods américains, a pris des dimensions quasi politiques.

Avec ses illustrations vieillottes, originalement publiées dans Vogue Magazine au cours des années 1930, French Caribbean Cuisine possède l'élégance d'un album. Il obéit à une construction rigoureuse allant des amuse-gueules aux boissons, que je laisse au lecteur le soin d'apprécier. Il ne s'agit pas d'une collection de recettes de grand-mères, compliquées et impossibles à réaliser au quotidien. Il ne s'agit pas non plus de recettes touristiques, hâtives et superficielles. À la fois élaborées et accessibles, celles qui sont présentées ici puisent leur originalité dans des secrets de famille gardés comme des secrets d'alcôve. Ou bien elles sont le fruit de rencontres avec des maîtres queux locaux. Ou encore elles représentent l'aboutisse- ment de recherches personnelles. Elles s'ancrent dans la modernité. Elles ne renient pas les meilleures traditions.

Bref, elles sont la vitrine culinaire de terres attachantes, complexes et diverses, mal connues aux États-Unis, mais qui méritent le détour.

À tous les gourmets et à tous les curieux épris de saveurs nouvelles, je souhaite donc « Bon appétit » !

Maryse Condé
Écrivain

Préface

I like to repeat it without false modesty: after some fifteen books, I still do not know if I am a good writer, whereas without possible doubt, I know that I am an excellent cook. For decades, I have been regaling my husband, my children, my guests. One of my dreams that—among others—will never come true, would be to own a restaurant where I would create the menu according to my whims, my encounters, my discoveries, here and there in the course of my travels, or simply when visiting friends, and which I would fashion with my own imagination. I would be sure to marry table and literature. For dessert, we would with relish eat poems; for coffee, we would enjoy savor excerpts from novels; after eating, we would without pedantry exchange opinions on novelistic techniques and various narrative strategies.

My mother, the daughter of a cook who hired her services out by the year, probably did not see things with such romanticism, and insisted that an intelligent woman is hopeless in the kitchen. Therefore during stays in France, deprived of her maids who had remained in Guadeloupe, she fed the family with hard-boiled eggs, canned peas and sardines in oil. I dispute the validity of such an elitist concept. For me, cooking is an art that requires as much creativity and audacity as writing. As with literature, one must invent. It is necessary to challenge the guest/reader without ever being afraid to innovate, experiment at the risk of surprising, or even shocking him before winning his approval. For me, the art of cooking can also be compared to painting: add green pepper dices to a dish, mix in kernels of golden corn, garnish it with a slice of red hot pepper, flavor rice with saffron with the aim of completing a perfect palette of color. Sacrilege? I have never been able to contemplate a Jackson Pollock painting without my mouth watering. "Abstract expressionism" one says? For me, it is not so abstract.

That is why I did not hesitate long before agreeing to write a preface for Stéphanie Ovide's book. She was affording me the opportunity to free an unsatisfied and unknown side of myself, hidden under novels, theater plays, articles of literary criticism, classes, and lectures.

French West-Indian cuisine is a mosaic. It is an invitation to travel, since this place, meandering along a mosaic peopling, is located at the crossroads of three traditions. Fed with "roots," "peas," cheap cuts of pork (muzzles, ears, tails), salted codfish and smoked herring, African slaves did not just fill stomachs that were left perpetually empty by the negligence of their masters, they also set the foundations of the culinary edifice. Europeans and Indians, who came to supplement the servile workforce after the abolition of slavery, added the colors and flavors borrowed from their own lands of origin and completed the culinary tradition. In the Caribbean, Martinique and Guadeloupe have the particularity of having been—for better or worse—colonized by the French, that is to say by people excessively in love with food. France, as we know, has conferred an almost religious dimension to proper eating. Chefs are revered as high priests. The Gault and Millau (which has nothing to do with the modest and practical concerns of the Zagat Survey) figures as the Bible. Traditionally washed down with wines judiciously chosen to enhance the variety of tastes, the festive meal lasts for hours. And it is not a coincidence that in France, the struggle against "bad eating," symbolized by MacDonald's and other American fast foods, has reached quasi-political dimensions.

With its old-fashioned illustrations, originally published in *Vogue* during the thirties, *French Caribbean Cuisine* has the elegance of an album. It follows a rigorous construction from appetizers to drinks that I entrust the reader to appreciate. It is not a collection of grandmothers' recipes, complicated and impossible to make on a day-to-day basis. Nor is it tourist-oriented, ready-made and superficial. Elaborate and accessible at the same time, the recipes presented here draw their originality from family secrets, jealously safeguarded for generations. Others are the fruit of encounters with local master chefs. Or they represent the outcome of personal research. They are rooted in modernity. They do not break with the best traditions. In short, they are the culinary showcases of fascinating lands, complex and diverse, quite unknown in the United States, but which are worth the journey.

To all gourmets and to the curious in love with new flavors, "Bon appétit!"

Maryse Condé
Writer

Contents

Introduction

Creole cuisine is about tropical colors, spicy flavors, and fresh tasty produce. Each cuisine is influenced by its history and geographic location and the Caribbean Islands are no exception. Although the cooking ingredients are common to all the archipelago of the West Indies, there are great variations among the English, Spanish, and French islands.

The archipelago of the West Indies is a long chain of islands that form an arc from Central to South America. It is made up of greater and lesser Antilles including Martinique, Guadeloupe, and its dependencies Les Saintes, Saint Martin, Saint Barthélémy, Marie Galante, and Desirade. Lined with deep clam bays, blue creeks surrounded by palm trees and sea grape vines, long beaches with golden sands, peaceful coves of limpid water, and jagged coastlines, these islands represent an ideal place for tourists and gourmet food.

The French West Indies offers a delightful and refined cuisine greatly influenced by consecutive waves of immigration. The arrival of the *Caraibes*, then of the Spaniards, Dutch, Africans, Indians, Chinese, and finally the French resulted in an eclectic population and culinary tradition, which includes tasteful dishes with a unique mélange of flavors. Among them is the cassava meal inherited from the first inhabitants, the *Caraibes*, the *Soupe à Congo*, *Bébélé*, and *Accras* brought by the African slaves; and the *Colombo* cherished by the Indian workers. The *Fish Blaff* was brought by the Dutch who came to the Island in 1634.

The Creole culinary tradition is epitomized by the annual Festival of *Cuisinières* or Cooks. Founded in 1916 in Pointe-à-Pitre, Guadeloupe, this festival celebrated from July to October pays tribute to Saint Laurent, the patron of cooks. All the best cooks of the islands wear the traditional Creole costume made of Madras fabric and beautiful jewelry to attend mass where savory traditional dishes are blessed. Then, they stroll down the streets forming an unprecedented colorful parade. In this warm and euphoric atmosphere, everybody has a great time dancing on the frenzy rhythm of the biguine, merengue, and mazurka.

This book attempts to capture the spirit of this colorful and subtle cuisine. It includes recipes collected among the best cooks of the islands and well-kept family secrets. A number of recipes are specialties of a particular island such as the *Tourment D'amour* from les Saintes, the *Hot Cocoa* from Martinique and the *Gateau Fouetté* from Guadeloupe. However, most traditional dishes can be found in all the French West Indies. With a constant concern of authenticity I have spent many hours researching and cooking with domestic cooks, fruit and vegetable merchants, and traveling in all the French islands to give you a real taste and appreciation of what French Creole cuisine is about.

The extensive glossary of culinary terms will help familiarize you with the various exotic fruits, vegetables, and fish. This book also includes a list of websites specializing in Caribbean products and spices.

Interestingly, French Creole recipes are increasingly found on French tables, which show an ever-growing interest in tropical and exotic flavors. In New York more and more bars offer the traditional *Ti Punch* next to the Brazilian *Caiperinia*. Magazines like French *Elle*, *Gourmet*, or *Condé Nast Traveler* regularly feature recipes from Guadeloupe and Martinique such as the *Blanc-Manger*, the *Coconut Flan*, or the *Chicken Colombo*. Starting a meal with some *accras* and a *planteur* can only bring a smile to your lips and warm-up to your evenings. French Creole cuisine is about fun, sun, and color. This book will offer you a wonderful experience incorporating all your senses.

Festivals

Carnival starts on Epiphany (January 6th) and runs through Ash Wednesday (6 weeks before Easter) with new events each Sunday. All the French islands celebrate this event.

The Fish and Sea Festival
on April 15th is celebrated on the beach with boat races, crab races, and parties.

La Fête des Cuisinières
(Festival of Cooks) takes place mid-August. During this event about 250 cooks from the Woman's Cooking Association wear traditional costumes and jewels and parade throughout the streets of Pointe-à-Pitre in Guadeloupe. A large banquet of the most delicious food is offered.

Fête du Gwo Ka
(Festival of the Big Drum) is during the month of July where the best Gwo Ka bands play around towns.

The Old Creole Song Festival
during the month of October revives the traditional songs of the French islands.

Bernard Lamotte/© Vogue, Condé Nast Publications Inc.

Glossary

Accras, served as appetizers, are fritters made with codfish or vegetables such as *giraumon* or tropical pumpkin and taro.

Allspice or *bois d'Indes* is a spice originally from Jamaica that looks like black pepper and adds delicious flavor to any dish.

Almond essence or extract is often used in crêpes, fruit fritters, and sweet drinks. A few drops suffice to delicately flavor a dessert.

Angostura Aromatic Bitters, first manufactured in 1830, has been used in Jamaica to add a refreshing twist to many drinks and punches.

Avocado, a fruit found in the French Caribbean islands, is very close to the Florida avocado. Pear shaped with a shiny green skin, it has a yellow and bright green flesh.

Bébélé is a specialty of Marie-Galante with a strong African influence. Traditionally made with tripe, pigtail, *dombrés* and *poyos*, it can also be prepared with shellfish.

Blaff is a poaching technique inherited from Holland. It named for the sound made by the ingredients when they are dropped in the pan.

Boudin is a sausage stuffed with a mix of pork blood, bread, and spices. It is the most popular dish in the French Caribbean islands and is served as an appetizer. Fish and conch boudin are increasingly popular.

Bouquet Garni is the base of French Creole cuisine. It includes sprigs of parsley, thyme, and bay leaf attached by a string of grass. For convenience, each herb is described separately in the ingredient list. However, to get closer to the original taste it is preferable to use the traditional *bouquet garni*.

Breadfruit is a large green fruit, 8 to 10 inches in diameter, with rough evenly green marked skin. It has the consistency of potatoes and is both nutritious and delicious. It is in season in July and August.

Cassava or *manioc* is a long brown root vegetable. There are two varieties of cassava, sweet and bitter. In the French Caribbean, bitter cassava is used to make flour. The sweet cassava is used for cooking.

Christophene (*cho-cho* or *chayote*) belongs to the melon family and was originally found in Cuba and Jamaica. Green or cream, this pear-shaped fruit is furrowed and slightly prickly, measuring between 4 and 6 inches long. Peeling the fruit leaves a sticky white substance on the hands that is harmless and easily washed off. Used mostly as a vegetable.

Cinnamon is mainly used in its powder form to flavor desserts.

Coconut is the large round fruit of a palm tree. When fresh and ripe, a clear sweet and tasty water is extracted from the shell. It is traditionally drunk for breakfast. Once halved a creamy white flesh can be detached easily from the shell. The dry and brown coconut is commonly found throughout the United Sates. A hammer can be used to open the shell.

Colombo is a traditional dish originally brought by the Indian community in the nineteenth century, after the abolition of slavery. It is a stew spiced with a powder made of curry, ground mustard grains, cumin, masala, and turmeric. Colombo powder can be found at Creoleshop.com.

Conch or *lambi* is a giant shellfish with spiral shell. The flesh is beaten until tender before cooking. The conch is a delicacy found throughout the French Caribbean islands. It can usually be purchased in Chinatown markets.

Crabs have a very strong and tasty flavor. The most common crabs in the French Caribbean are land crabs. They can be substituted with sea crabs in most recipes.

Crayfish are close to lobsters without claws. Their refined flesh makes them a delicacy in the French Caribbean.

Danquits are small breads fried in oil. They can be eaten plain or serve as bread to make sandwiches.

Dombrés are little balls of dough boiled in soups. They are similar to the knepffes of Strasbourg in France.

Giraumon is from the pumpkin family. It is very close to the Chinese or tropical pumpkin. It has a dark green skin with white spots. The flesh is bright yellow.

Guava is a round yellow fruit, 2 to 3 inches in diameter with a thick edible skin. Numerous small seeds are embedded in the soft pulp. There are two varieties of guava found in the French Caribbean: the pink and the white flesh. Guavas have a very high nutritive value and are good source of iron.

Langoustes are from the lobster family. They have an extremely refined taste.

Limes are very tasty fruits found in the French Caribbean and are used in all the traditional dishes. They are 4 to 6 inches in diameter, bright green, and perfectly round.

Malanga is a root vegetable with a light pink flesh, very close to taro root.

Mango is a one-seeded, thin-skinned oval or round fruit. The flesh is orange-yellow. There are over 1,000 varieties of mango in the French Caribbean. The most common are the *julie, pomme, figue*, and *greffée*.

Nutmeg, originally from the Moluccas Islands, is traditionally used in the French West Indies in pastries and jams.

Okra or *gombo* is a green ribbed vegetable about 5 to 6 inches long.

Papaya (papaw) is a melon-like fruit. When ripe and yellow-golden, it is eaten as a fruit. When green, the unripe fruit becomes a vegetable very close in flavor to a squash.

Pigtails are used in many dishes for their taste and texture. They have to be cleaned thoroughly before cooking. The most popular dish is the *Migan et Fruit a Pain* or Breadfruit Migan.

Plantains belong to the banana family. Plantains are used when ripe and yellow in the French islands and are cooked like vegetables.

Pois de bois, *pois d'Angole*, Congo peas, or pigeon peas are used extensively throughout the Caribbean islands. They are all from the same black-eyed pea family.

Poyo is the name of any small unripe green banana. They have a very thick skin that needs to be removed with a sharp knife. *Poyos* are used as vegetables.

Red Butter, or *beurre rouge*, commonly used in everyday Creole cuisine, is obtained by mixing *roucou* seeds with butter.

Roucou is a red seed with a delicate flavor. The first inhabitants of the Caribbean used it as an antidote for poisonous plants. Soaked in oil for several days, it gives a vivid color to any dish, especially the *court-bouillon*.

Rum agricole, or white rum is most popular throughout the French Caribbean islands. It offers unique fruit and spiced flavors.

Rum vieux or old rum is aged rum for 15 years or more. Used in cocktails or as a digestif, the French Caribbean old rum is known to be the best in the Caribbean archipelago.

Scotch Bonnet pepper, *habanero*, or *puments* are the most commonly grown varieties of pepper grown in the Caribbean region. They are from the *Capsicum chinense* family, which comes in many forms of pods ranging from round to top-shaped, long, or lantern-shaped. Colors can range from white to yellow, orange, red, or brown. They flavor most dishes.

Spotted tuna or *bonito* is a robust chunky fish. The flesh is coarse and dark. The roe is a special delicacy.

Star apple or *carambole* is a five-winged translucent yellow or yellow-green fruit. It has a very distinctive star shape when cross-sectioned.

Sweet potato or *patate douce* is often used as a side dish. This enlarged tuberous root is 5 to 6 inches long and has a pink or orange flesh.

Taro *(igname)* is a tropical root vegetable usually the size of a large potato, with brown, hairy skin and white, pink, or purple flesh. It has a light texture and pleasant flavor.

Tripe is a common ingredient in many dishes influenced by African culinary traditions including the *Bébélé*.

Vanilla with its strong fragrance is used exclusively in desserts such as cakes, cream, pastries, jams, flans, and ice creams. To extract the full flavor, the bean is halved and the pulp is grated. Brown sugar can be flavored with fresh vanilla.

Vivaneau from the red snapper family is considered the most refined fish. They have a deep rose skin and red fins. They measure 2 to 3 feet in length and weighs from 30 to 40 pounds. The flesh is white and fluffy.

Appetizers

The Creole *apéritif* (the time for pre-dinner drinks and snacks) is directly inspired by French culinary tradition and culture. Served with the traditional Ti Punch (see page 215), traditional appetizers include codfish or vegetable fritters (*accras*), stuffed crabs or clams and finally the delicious spicy *Boudin Creole*. This last delicacy is a blood sausage flavored with a mixture of tropical spices and pimiento. It is a very complex recipe involving many days of preparation, which is why I did not include it in this book. The most savory *boudins*, however, are the ones cooked locally. My favorite is the *boudin* from Saint-Félix on the road to Sainte-Anne in Guadeloupe where a lady has been making and selling it every week for over 10 years. Recently, fish and conch *boudins* have started to appear on French Caribbean tables. Getting away from the traditional *Ti Punch-accras-boudin*, French Caribbean cuisine offers a great variety of appetizers. From my Uncle Ary's fish rillettes to Mamie's onion pie, I remember these elaborate appetizers being served during carefree and seemingly endless *apéritifs* punctuated by laughs, music and lively conversations.

Appetizers

Avocado Féroce

Avocado Fritters

Avocado Charlotte

Avocado Omelette

Bonne-Maman Fish Croquettes

Codfish Chiquetaille

Codfish Fritters

Crab Puffs

Stuffed Clams

Stuffed Crabs

Uncle Ary's Fish Rillettes

Fish Crêpes Saintoise

Croque Creole

Lisette's Eggplant

Mamie's Onion Pie

Mamie Zea's Giraumon Pie

Plantain with Bacon

Vegetable Fritters

Coconut Bites

Avocado Féroce

4 servings

2 cups peeled and chopped Florida avocados
1/2 cup Codfish Chiquetaille (page 34)
3/4 cup cassava (manioc) meal
1 cup peeled and thinly sliced cucumber
1/4 teaspoon Scotch Bonnet Pepper Confit (page 198)

Mash the avocado with a fork. Stir in the codfish, cassava meal, and cucumber.

Roll into 4-inch diameter balls. Add additional cassava meal if too sticky. Season with Scotch Bonnet Pepper Confit.

Serve at once.

Avocado Fritters

6 servings

1/2 cup sifted flour
1 cup sunflower oil
2 eggs
1 tablespoon salt
2 cups peeled and quartered avocado

In a bowl combine the flour, 1 tablespoon of the oil, eggs, and salt. Stir in 2 table-spoons of water and mix to form a thick creamy dough (adjust the amount of water if necessary).

In a frying pan heat the remaining oil over medium heat. Dip each avocado quarter in batter and cook in oil, 4 or 5 at a time, until golden brown.

Drain each fritter in a colander lined with paper towel. Serve hot.

Avocado Charlotte

4 servings

3 Florida avocados, peeled and diced
1/4 cup freshly squeezed lime juice
4 sheets or 1 packet Knox unflavored gelatine
1 cup sour cream
1 tablespoon salt
1 tablespoon pepper
2 limes, sliced
4 sprigs parsley

In a blender, combine the avocados and lime juice. Puree.

Soak the gelatine sheets in warm water for 10 minutes. Drain. If using powdered gelatine, combine with 4 cups of warm water for 5 minutes until thick.

In a large bowl, combine the avocado puree and gelatine. Fold in the sour cream. Season with salt and pepper.

Turn into a charlotte mold or a deep-sided dish. Refrigerate for 4 to 5 hours.

Soak the mold in hot water for a few minutes and turn into a serving dish.

Garnish with lime slices and parsley. Serve at once.

Avocado Omelette

4 servings

2 cups peeled and sliced Florida avocado
1 tablespoon chopped chives
1 tablespoon chopped parsley
1 teaspoon fresh thyme
8 eggs
1 teaspoon salt
1/2 teaspoon pepper
4 tablespoons butter

Mash the avocado with a fork. Stir in the chives, parsley, and thyme.

Beat the eggs in a bowl and season with salt and pepper. Add half of the avocado to raw eggs.

Melt butter in a pan over low heat and pour in the eggs. Once the eggs are cooked, spread on the second half of the avocado puree. Fold the omelette in half and slide onto a serving plate.

Serve hot.

Bonne-Maman Fish Croquettes

4 servings

4 tablespoons chopped chives
2 tablespoons chopped parsley
2 tablespoons fresh thyme
1/2 teaspoon chopped Scotch Bonnet pepper
1/2 teaspoon salt
1/4 teaspoon pepper
2 pounds fresh tuna
2 cups Béchamel Sauce with Eggs (page 192)
1/2 cup sunflower oil
1 cup bread crumbs

In a large saucepan, combine 4 cups of water, chives, parsley, thyme, Scotch Bonnet pepper, salt, and pepper. Add the fish. Bring to a boil and simmer for 20 minutes. Drain the fish. Skin, bone, and puree the fish.

Prepare the béchamel sauce. Add the fish and stir well. Let cool.

Form 4-inch long cylinders with the fish mixture. Heat the oil in a large frying pan over medium heat. Dip each cylinder in the bread crumbs. Fry 1 minute on each side until golden. Drain in a colander lined with paper towels.

Serve warm on a bed of Creole Rice (page 75) with Sauce Chien (page 194).

Codfish Chiquetaille

6 servings

1/2 pound salted codfish
1 cup sunflower oil
1 cup peeled and chopped onion
2 tablespoons white wine vinegar
2 tablespoons chopped chives
1 tablespoon peeled and crushed garlic
1 tablespoon chopped parsley

Preheat the oven to 350 degrees F. Place the codfish in an ovenproof dish and bake for 15 minutes. Remove from the oven and let it cool.

In glass jar, combine the oil, onion, vinegar, chives, garlic, and parsley.

Prepare the codfish. Remove the bones and skin and crumble the flesh in tiny pieces. Add to the glass container and close. Let the fish marinate for at least 1 day before serving.

Prepared this way, the codfish can be kept in a refrigerator up to a week.

Serve with Avocado Féroce (page 29).

Codfish Fritters

6 servings

1/2 pound salted codfish
1 cup flour
1 teaspoon salt
1/2 teaspoon pepper
2 eggs, beaten
1 tablespoon chopped chives
1 teaspoon peeled and crushed garlic
1 tablespoon fresh thyme
1 cup sunflower oil

In a large saucepan, bring 2 cups of water to a boil. Add the codfish and cook 30 minutes. Drain in colander and let it cool.

Prepare the batter in a large bowl. Combine flour, salt, and pepper with 1 cup of water. Add the eggs and stir until creamy.

Prepare the codfish. Remove the bones and skin and crumble the flesh in tiny pieces. Add the codfish, chives, garlic, and thyme to the batter. Stir until smooth. Cover and let it rest for 1 hour.

Heat the oil in a saucepan. Drop 3 to 4 tablespoons of batter in oil and cook until golden brown. Drain in colander.

Serve hot.

Crab Puffs

6 servings

3 slices stale bread
2 tablespoons sunflower oil
2 cloves garlic, crushed
1/2 cup peeled and chopped onion
1/4 cup chopped chives
1/2 teaspoon chopped Scotch Bonnet pepper
2 cans (7 ounces each) crabmeat
1 lime, squeezed
1 teaspoon salt
1 teaspoon pepper
1 Flaky Pastry (page 162)
1/2 cup flour
2 egg yolks, beaten

Soak the bread in 1 cup water for 1 hour. Drain with the palm of your hands and puree.

Prepare the stuffing. Heat the oil in a large saucepan. Add the garlic, onion, chives, and Scotch Bonnet pepper. Brown 2 to 3 minutes over medium heat. Stir in the crabmeat, lime juice, bread, salt, and pepper. Simmer over medium heat for 20 minutes.

Preheat the oven to 350 degrees F. Flour your hands. Roll the pastry into a large circle and sprinkle with 2 tablespoons flour. Cut out 24 disks with a 4-inch diameter glass.

Place 1 teaspoon of stuffing at the center of a disk and cover with a second disk. Seal with your finger. Repeat. Place on a baking sheet. Brush with egg yolks and bake for 20 to 30 minutes until puffed and golden.

Serve warm.

Variation
Meat Puffs:
Substitute 2 pounds ground beef for the crabmeat.
Eliminate the lime juice and simmer for 30 minutes instead of 20.

Stuffed Crabs

6 servings

12 crabs (about 5 to 6 pounds)
1 cup freshly squeezed lime juice
1 pound bread, torn
2 tablespoons oil
1 cup diced chives
1 tablespoon peeled and crushed garlic
1 teaspoon black pepper
3 cups bread crumbs
1 cup chopped parsley

Preheat the oven to 400 degrees F. Wash and clean the crabs under tap water. Rub them with lime juice.

Bring 6 cups of water to a boil. Add the crabs and poach for 10 minutes. Drain. Remove the flesh from the crabs shells. Reserve the shells.

Soak the bread in water for 30 minutes then drain in a colander. Heat the oil in saucepan; add the chives, garlic, pepper, and the crabmeat until brown. Fill the crab shells with the stuffing and place them on a baking tray. Sprinkle the top with bread crumbs and garnish with parsley. Bake for 25 minutes.

Serve warm.

Stuffed Clams

6 servings

12 medium-size clams, cleaned
2 tablespoons diced chives
2 tablespoons fresh thyme
4 tablespoons chopped parsley

Stuffing
1/2 cup stale sliced bread
1/4 cup oil
2 tablespoons diced chives
1 teaspoon peeled and crushed garlic
2 tablespoons chopped parsley
1/2 teaspoon salt
1/4 teaspoon pepper
1 chopped red Scotch Bonnet pepper
1 cup bread crumbs

Combine the clams, chives, thyme, and parsley in a large saucepan. Cover and cook over medium heat until the clams are opened. Remove the clams and reserve the liquid.

Delicately detach the flesh from each clamshell and chop finely. Reserve the shells in an ovenproof dish.

Soak the bread in the cooking liquid until tender.

Prepare the stuffing. Combine oil, chives, garlic, and parsley in a high-sided frying pan and cook on low heat for 5 minutes. Stir in the clams and drained bread. Add salt and pepper. Cook for 15 minutes.

Preheat oven to 350 degrees F. Fill each clam shell with the stuffing and top with a piece of Scotch Bonnet pepper.

Sprinkle with bread crumbs. Bake 10 minutes.

Serve hot with a tomato or cucumber salad.

Uncle Ary's Fish Rillettes

4 servings

8 tablespoons chopped parsley
3 tablespoons thyme
6 tablespoons chopped chives
1/2 teaspoon salt
1/2 teaspoon pepper
1 1/4 cups cleaned white fish
1/2 cup chopped smoked fish
1 cup butter, melted
4 tablespoons olive oil
2 egg yolks
1 clove garlic, crushed
1/4 teaspoon cinnamon
1/4 teaspoon nutmeg
1/3 teaspoon seeded and chopped Scotch Bonnet pepper
1 cup cornichons
8 slices bread
1 lime, halved

In a large saucepan, combine 6 tablespoons of the parsley, the thyme, 4 tablespoons of the chives, salt, pepper, and white fish. Add 6 cups of water. Bring to a boil and simmer for 25 minutes. Drain. Bone and skin the fish.

Crumble the flesh over a large bowl. Stir in the smoked fish. Add the butter, olive oil, egg yolks, garlic, cinnamon, nutmeg, and Scotch Bonnet pepper. Stir well with a fork until smooth.

Line a loaf pan with foil paper. Turn the fish into the pan. Refrigerate for 24 hours.

Turn into a serving dish. Sprinkle with the remaining 2 tablespoons of parsley and 2 tablespoons of chives. Decorate with cornichons.

Serve on toasted bread topped with drops of lime juice.

Fish Crêpes Saintoises

8 servings

4 tablespoons chopped chives
2 tablespoons chopped parsley
2 tablespoons fresh thyme
1/2 teaspoon chopped Scotch Bonnet pepper
1/2 teaspoon salt
1/4 teaspoon pepper
4 pounds swordfish
2 cups Béchamel Sauce (page 191)
Crêpe batter (page 171)
3 egg yolks
2 cups bread crumbs
1 tablespoon oil

In a large saucepan, combine 4 cups of water, chives, parsley, thyme, Scotch Bonnet pepper, salt, and pepper. Add the fish. Bring to a boil and simmer for 20 minutes. Drain the fish. Skin, bone, and purée.

Prepare Béchamel Sauce (page 191). Add the fish and stir well.

Prepare the crêpes.

Preheat the oven to 350 degrees F. Place a tablespoon of fish sauce at the bottom of each crêpe. Fold over two side edges then roll. Secure with a drop of water spread along the edge. Brush with egg yolks. Coat with bread crumbs.

Grease a large shallow baking dish. Place the crêpes next to each other. Bake for 35 minutes.

Serve warm.

Croque Creole

4 servings

2 teaspoons butter
4 slices bread
1 cup peeled and sliced Florida avocados
1/4 teaspoon salt
1/4 teaspoon pepper
1/4 pound sliced boiled ham or turkey
2 cups peeled and sliced tomatoes
1/4 teaspoon sliced Scotch Bonnet pepper
1/2 cup grated Swiss or Gruyère cheese

In a large frying pan, melt the butter on low heat. Add the bread and cook on both sides until brown. Preheat the oven to 350 degrees F.

Arrange the bread in an ovenproof dish. On each slice of bread place avocado, salt, pepper, meat, tomatoes, and Scotch Bonnet peppers. Sprinkle with cheese.

Bake 10 minutes. Serve hot with a mixed green salad.

Lisette's Eggplant

6 servings

1 pound eggplants
1/2 cup flour
2 eggs, beaten
1/2 teaspoon salt
1/2 cup sunflower oil

Clean the eggplants under cold tap water. Wipe with paper towels. Cut into 1/2-inch thick slices.

In a large shallow dish, combine the flour, eggs, and salt with 1/2 cup of water. Stir until smooth and creamy. Coat the eggplants with the batter.

Heat the oil in a large frying pan over medium heat. Fry the eggplants 2 minutes on each side. Drain in a colander lined with paper towels.

Serve warm with a Ti Punch (page 215).

Mamie's Onion Pie

6 servings

1 tablespoon oil
1/2 pound diced bacon
3 pounds onions, peeled and sliced
2 tablespoons milk
1 recipe Short Crust Pastry (page 161)
1 cup grated Swiss or Gruyère cheese

Heat the oil in a large saucepan. Stir in the bacon, onions, and milk. Cook over low heat for 15 to 20 minutes, stirring occasionally. Preheat the oven to 350 degrees F.

Line a pie tin with crust. Fill with the onions and bacon. Sprinkle with grated cheese.
Bake for 20 to 25 minutes.

Serve warm.

Mamie Zea's Giraumon Pie

6 servings

6 teaspoons butter
2 cups peeled and sliced onions
1 clove garlic, crushed
1 cup chopped parsley
1 pound giraumon (Chinese pumpkin), peeled and diced
4 eggs
2 cups chopped boiled ham
1 recipe Short Crust Pastry (page 161)
1 cup grated Swiss cheese

Preheat oven to 300 degrees F. Heat 4 teaspoons of the butter in a large saucepan. Stir in the onions, garlic, and parsley. Brown over medium heat.

Add the giraumon and 1/2 cup of water. Simmer for 45 minutes until soft. Stir in the eggs and ham.

Line a 16-inch pan with crust. Sprinkle with grated cheese and remaining butter. Bake for 30 minutes.

Serve warm with a mixed green salad.

Plantain with Bacon

4 servings

4 cups peeled and thickly sliced (about 1 inch x 1 inch)
  ripe yellow plantains
1 pound bacon, sliced

Preheat the oven to 350 degrees F.

Roll a slice of bacon around each piece of plantain. Secure with a toothpick. Arrange on a baking sheet. Bake 10 to 15 minutes.

Serve hot.

Vegetable Fritters

3 cups peeled and grated malanga
1 cup peeled and grated giraumon (Chinese pumpkin)
2 tablespoons chopped chives
1 tablespoon fresh thyme
1 tablespoon peeled and crushed garlic
1 tablespoon salt
1/2 tablespoon pepper
1 teaspoon chopped Scotch Bonnet pepper (optional)
1 cup sunflower oil

In a large bowl combine the malanga and pumpkin. Add the chives, thyme, garlic, salt, pepper, and Scotch Bonnet pepper. Stir until obtaining a creamy batter.

Heat the oil in a saucepan. Drop 3 to 4 tablespoons of batter at a time in the oil and cook until golden brown. Drain in colander lined with paper towels.

Serve hot.

Coconut Bites

4 servings

1 coconut in the shell
3 tablespoons butter
3 tablespoons salt

Beat the coconut shell with a hammer until it breaks into pieces. With a sharp knife remove the pulp from the shell. Break the flesh into 1-inch bites.

Melt butter in a frying pan. Stir in the coconut and brown over medium heat for 10 minutes. Sprinkle with salt.

Serve warm.

Soups and Salads

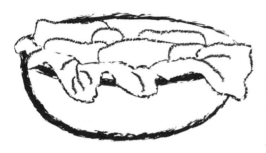

One might mistakenly think that Caribbean weather is too warm to eat soup. Interestingly, the temperature drops by a few degrees after sunset during the *Hivernage* or winter, from November to the end of January. During this season, a warm and tasteful soup is most appreciated at dinnertime. My favorite is Aunt Babeth's lentil soup, especially when she generously adds some crème fraîche and grated Gruyère cheese to it. *Congo Soup* or *Soup Zabitan*, introduced by Africans during the time of slavery, offer a copious and healthy meal when preceded by a simple salad.

Salads, colorfully and artfully arranged, offer a fresh and welcome soothing when eaten with spicy appetizers. The fresh produce including avocados, lettuce, green papayas, cucumbers and tomatoes are dressed with a delicate garlic and lime vinaigrette. One of my father's tricks is to grate the cucumbers lengthwise, making them easier to digest. For a complete meal, crudités can be served with hard-boiled eggs.

Soups and Salads

Traditional Pumpkin Soup

Pumpkin and Coconut Soup

Soup Zabitan

Babeth's Lentil Soup

Breadfruit Soup

Clam Soup

Congo Soup

Creole Salad

Avocado Cucumber Salad

Christophenes Salad

Lime Cucumber Salad

Mango Rougail

Okra

Papaya Salad

Spinach Salad

Sweet Potato Salad

Traditional Pumpkin Soup

4 servings

1 pound giraumon (Chinese pumpkin), peeled, seeded and diced
2 tablespoons salt
1 1/2 cups milk
1/2 cup white or brown rice
1 tablespoon brown sugar
1/3 cup butter
1 cup croutons

In a saucepan, combine 2 cups of water with the pumpkin and salt. Simmer for 40 minutes until tender. Drain. Turn the pumpkin into a blender and pureé.

In a large saucepan, combine the pumpkin puree with milk and rice. Simmer over low heat for 10 to 15 minutes. Stir in the brown sugar and butter. Simmer for another 30 minutes.

Turn into a soup tureen and serve hot with croutons.

Pumpkin and Coconut Soup

4 servings

1/4 cup butter
1 cup peeled and chopped onion
1 pound giraumon (Chinese pumpkin),
    peeled, seeded, and diced
1 tablespoon ground ginger
2 tablespoons curry powder
1 can (28 ounces) coconut milk
1/4 cup sour cream
1/3 cup freshly squeezed lime juice
2 tablespoons salt
2 tablespoons pepper
1/4 cup grated coconut
2 tablespoons grated lime peel

In a large saucepan melt the butter over low heat. Add the onion and cook for 10 minutes. Add the pumpkin and let simmer for 5 minutes. Season with the ginger and curry powder.

Cover with 1 cup of water, stir, and simmer for 30 minutes. Stir in the coconut milk and simmer for another 20 minutes.

Turn the soup into a blender and mix until smooth and creamy. Stir in the sour cream and lime juice. Season with salt and pepper.

Turn into in a soup tureen or individual bowls. Sprinkle with grated coconut and lime peel.

Serve hot.

Soup Zabitan

6 servings

1/4 cup sunflower oil
2 pounds beef brisket, diced
2 cups peeled and diced sweet potatoes
1 cup peeled and sliced cucumber
2 cups peeled, seeded, and diced pumpkin
2 cups chopped cabbage
1 cup peeled and chopped turnip
1 cup peeled and chopped carrot
2 cups peeled and chopped taro
2 tablespoons salt
1 tablespoon pepper
1 cup peeled and chopped celery
1 teaspoon chopped Scotch Bonnet pepper

In a large saucepan heat the oil. Stir in the meat, potatoes, cucumber, pumpkin, cabbage, turnip, carrot, and taro. Cover and simmer for 10 to 15 minutes, stirring occasionally.

Add 6 cups of water, salt, pepper, celery, and Scotch Bonnet pepper. Simmer over low heat for 1 1/2 hours.

Serve hot.

Babeth's Lentil Soup

4 servings

1 pound lentils
1 teaspoon salt
2 branches thyme
3 tablespoons chopped chives
1/4 cup sour cream
2 tablespoons butter
3 tablespoons chopped parsley
1 cup grated swiss or Gruyère cheese

In a large saucepan combine the lentils with 6 cups of water. Season with salt, thyme, and chives. Bring to a boil and simmer over medium heat for 45 minutes.

Purée in a blender. Turn into a soup tureen. Stir in the sour cream and butter. Sprinkle with parsley and grated cheese.

Serve hot.

Breadfruit Soup

4 servings

4 cups peeled and diced breadfruit
2 tablespoons salt
2 tablespoons oil
3 cups peeled and sliced onion
2 cups chopped and seeded tomatoes
1 tablespoon pepper
1 celery stalk

Combine the breadfruit with 4 cups of water and salt in a large saucepan. Simmer over medium heat for 30 minutes until tender. Turn into a blender and mix until smooth and creamy. Pour back into the large saucepan.

In a skillet, heat the oil over low heat. Stir in the onion and tomatoes and simmer for 30 minutes. Turn into the breadfruit soup.

Season with pepper and simmer over low heat for 15 minutes. Add the celery stalk 5 minutes before the end of cooking time.

Serve hot.

Clam Soup

6 servings

2 pounds clams, cleaned and brushed
2 tablespoons butter
4 cups peeled and chopped carrots
2 cups peeled and chopped leeks
1 cup chopped celery
2 cups peeled and sliced potatoes
1 cup chopped cabbage
3 cups peeled and chopped turnips
2 tablespoons salt
1/4 cup white or brown rice

In a saucepan, combine the clams and 6 cups of water. Bring to a boil and simmer over low heat for 10 to 15 minutes until the clams are open. Shell the clams and reserve the liquid.

In a large saucepan, heat the butter over medium heat. Add the carrots, leeks, celery, potatoes, cabbage, and turnips. Season with salt. Simmer over medium heat for 10 minutes.

Stir in the shelled clams and the liquid. Add the rice and cook for 1 hour over low heat.

Serve hot.

Congo Soup

4 servings

1/4 cup sunflower oil
1 pound smoked bacon
2 cups peeled and diced eggplants
2 cups peeled and diced yams
1 cup okra
2 cups green beans
2 cups kohlrabi
2 cups Congo peas
2 cups peeled and diced sweet potatoes
1 cup peeled and sliced cucumber
2 cups peeled, seeded, and diced pumpkin
2 cups chopped cabbage
1 cup peeled and chopped turnip
1 cup peeled and chopped carrot
2 cups peeled and chopped taro
2 cloves garlic, crushed
1 onion, peeled
1/4 teaspoon whole cloves
2 tablespoons salt
1 tablespoon pepper
1 cup peeled and chopped celery
1 teaspoon chopped Scotch Bonnet pepper

In a large saucepan heat the oil. Stir in the bacon, eggplants, yams, okra, green beans, kohlrabi, gangoo peas, sweet potatoes, cucumber, pumpkin, cabbage, turnip, carrot, and taro. Cover and simmer for 10 to 15 minutes, stirring occasionally.

Add 8 cups of water and the onion pricked with cloves. Season with salt, pepper, celery, and Scotch Bonnet pepper. Simmer over low heat for 1 1/2 hours until the soup becomes thick.

Serve hot.

Creole Salad

6 servings

4 cups cleaned and chopped lettuce
4 cups cleaned and sliced plum tomatoes
2 cups peeled and grated cucumbers
2 cups peeled and quartered Florida avocados
1 tablespoon freshly squeezed lime juice
2 teaspoons peeled and crushed garlic
2 tablespoons white wine vinegar
1/2 teaspoon salt
1/4 teaspoon pepper
4 tablespoons sunflower oil

In a flat serving dish form a bed of lettuce. Arrange the tomatoes in a circle on top of the lettuce and add the cucumbers at the center. Lay the avocados along the edge.

Add the lime juice on the cucumber.

Prepare the vinaigrette. In a bowl, combine the garlic, vinegar, salt, and pepper. Stir in the oil.

Pour the vinaigrette over the salad and serve.

Avocado Cucumber Salad

6 servings

2 pounds peeled and thinly sliced cucumber
1 pound peeled and thinly sliced Florida avocado
1/3 cup freshly squeezed lime juice
1 teaspoon peeled and crushed garlic
2 tablespoons olive oil
1/2 teaspoon salt
1/4 teaspoon pepper
2 tablespoons pine nuts

In a flat serving dish arrange the sliced cucumbers and the avocado. Sprinkle with lime juice, garlic, oil, salt, pepper, and pine nuts.

Serve chilled.

 # Christophene Salad

6 servings

2 teaspoons salt
4 cups peeled, cored, and chopped christophenes (chayote)
4 tablespoons sunflower oil
2 tablespoons white wine vinegar
1 tablespoon mayonnaise
1 clove garlic, crushed
1 teaspoon pepper
2 tablespoons chopped parsley

In a large saucepan combine 4 cups of water and 1 teaspoon of the salt. Bring to a boil. Add the christophenes and simmer for 20 minutes. Drain.

Prepare the vinaigrette in a small bowl. Stir the oil, vinegar, mayonnaise, garlic, remaining 1 teaspoon of salt, and pepper.

Combine the christophenes and vinaigrette in a large salad bowl. Sprinkle with parsley.

Serve at room temperature.

Lime Cucumber Salad

6 servings

2 pounds cucumber, peeled
1/3 cup freshly squeezed lime juice
1 teaspoon peeled and crushed garlic
2 tablespoons sunflower oil
1/2 teaspoon salt
1/4 teaspoon pepper

In a salad bowl, grate the cucumbers lengthwise with a grater. Add the lime juice and garlic. Stir in the oil, salt, and pepper. Refrigerate for 1 hour.

Serve with stuffed clams.

Mango Rougail

4 servings

3 unripe (green) mangoes
2 tablespoons chopped chives
1/2 cup peeled and chopped onion
1 clove garlic, crushed
1 tablespoon fresh thyme
1/3 cup sunflower oil
1 teaspoon salt
1 teaspoon pepper
1 teaspoon chopped Scotch Bonnet pepper

Peel and dice the mangoes. Turn into a large salad bowl with chives, onion, garlic, and thyme.

Season with oil, salt, pepper, and Scotch Bonnet pepper. Stir well.

Refrigerate for 1 hour.

Serve chilled.

Okra

4 servings

2 pounds okra, cleaned
1 tablespoon salt
2 tablespoons chopped parsley
1 tablespoon fresh thyme
2 tablespoons chopped chives
1 teaspoon peeled and crushed garlic
1 tablespoon freshly squeezed lime juice
1/2 teaspoon Scotch Bonnet pepper (optional)

In a large saucepan, cover the okra with water. Stir in salt, parsley, thyme, and chives. Bring to a boil and cook for 30 to 45 minutes until tender. Transfer to a shallow plate.

Just before serving, add garlic, lime juice and Scotch Bonnet pepper.

Serve warm.

Papaya Salad

6 servings

4 tablespoons sunflower oil
2 tablespoons white wine vinegar
1 tablespoon mayonnaise
1 clove garlic, crushed
1 teaspoon salt
1/2 teaspoon pepper
4 cups peeled, seeded, and grated unripe (green) papayas
2 tablespoons chopped parsley
2 tablespoons freshly squeezed lime juice

Prepare the vinaigrette in a small bowl. Combine the oil, vinegar, mayonnaise, garlic, salt, and pepper.

Combine the papayas and vinaigrette in a large salad bowl. Sprinkle with parsley and lime juice.

Serve at room temperature.

Spinach Salad

6 servings

3 pounds spinach, cleaned
1/4 cup chopped chives
3 hard-boiled eggs, peeled and halved
1/3 teaspoon salt
1/4 teaspoon pepper
1 teaspoon peeled and crushed garlic
2 tablespoons white wine vinegar
4 tablespoons sunflower oil

In a large saucepan bring 6 cups of water to a boil. Add spinach and cook for 10 minutes until tender. Drain and let cool. Transfer onto a flat serving plate. Sprinkle with chives.

Arrange the eggs around the spinach.

Prepare the vinaigrette. In a bowl combine salt, pepper, garlic, and vinegar. Stir in the oil.

Pour the vinaigrette over the spinach and serve at once.

Sweet Potato Salad

6 servings

1 pound sweet potatoes
2 tablespoons salt
1 cup peeled and sliced onion
4 tablespoons sunflower oil
2 tablespoons white wine vinegar
1 tablespoon mayonnaise
1 clove garlic, crushed
1/2 teaspoon pepper
1 tablespoon chopped Scotch Bonnet pepper (optional)
2 tablespoons chopped parsley

In a large saucepan, combine the sweet potatoes with water to cover and 1 1/2 tablespoons of the salt. Bring to a boil and simmer for 45 minutes. Drain.

Peel and slice the sweet potatoes. Turn in a salad bowl.

Prepare the vinaigrette in a small bowl. Stir the oil, vinegar, mayonnaise, garlic, the remaining 1/2 teaspoon salt, pepper, and Scotch Bonnet pepper. Pour over the salad. Sprinkle with parsley.

Serve warm.

Vegetables

Taro, malanga, sweet potato, christophene, plantain, or eggplant… there is such a great variety of flavorful tropical vegetables and so many delicious ways to prepare them, such as fluffy vegetable gratin with béchamel sauce, delicate soufflé and refined purée. Of all the Caribbean islands, Martinique and Guadeloupe offer the most complex and refined cuisine, influenced by the French culinary tradition. Applauded chef Francis Delage, who resides on the island of Saint Barthélémy and is author of *La Cuisine Des Iles*, took French Caribbean cuisine to its zenith and dedicated an entire volume of his book to vegetables.

Most Caribbean root vegetables are available throughout the United States. Although they all have the same dark brown skin, the color and aspect of the flesh and the taste vary considerably. Malanga have a gray-white skin whereas *igname* or taro are totally white and *patate douce* or sweet potatoes have a pink flesh.

For a casual meal, these root vegetables can be boiled in salted water, and go well with any cooked meat, poultry, or fish dish. My favorite is the Codfish *Chiquetaille* with an assortment of salted root vegetables and a drop of Scotch Bonnet Pepper *Confit*.

Vegetables

Creole Rice

Creole Fried Rice

Creole Risotto

Pumpkin Rice

Rice and Tomatoes

Saffron Rice

Red Beans and Rice

Red Beans with Coconut

Creole Red Beans

Codie's Breadfruit
   Croquettes

Breadfruit Fries

Breadfruit Migan

Breadfruit Soufflé

Christmas Pois de Bois

Cucumber Court Bouillon

Creole Ratatouille

Eggplant Cake with
   Tomato Sauce

Eggplant Gratin

Eggplant Purée

Baked Eggplant

Lolo's Stuffed Eggplant

Giraumonade

Lentil and Dombrés

Mamie's Yellow Bananas

Papaya Gratin

Papaya Soufflé

Sandra's Plantain Gratin

Plantain Gratin

Plantain Fries

Salted Taro

Salted Sweet Potatoes

Sweet Potatoes Fries

Taro Fries

Spinach à la Béchamel

Stuffed Christophenes

Creole Rice

6 servings

2 1/2 cups long-grain white rice
1 teaspoon salt
1 onion, peeled
1 branch parsley
1 branch thyme
1 carrot, peeled

Soak the rice in cold water for 15 minutes and drain.

In a large saucepan, bring 6 cups of water to a boil. Add salt, onion, parsley, thyme, and carrot. Add the rice and simmer over medium heat for 20 minutes.

Remove the onion, parsley, thyme, and carrot. Drain the rice in a colander. Rinse under cold running water. Drain again and turn into saucepan.

Simmer over low heat for 5 minutes until the rice grains are completely dry.

Creole Fried Rice

6 servings

1/4 cup sunflower oil
1 cup frozen mixed vegetables
1 clove garlic, crushed
1/2 cup peeled and chopped onion
1 tablespoon chopped chives
1/2 cup chopped Canadian bacon
1 cup long-grain white rice
1 teaspoon salt
1/2 teaspoon pepper

Heat the oil in a large saucepan. Stir in the mixed vegetables, garlic, onion, chives, and bacon. Brown 10 to 15 minutes over medium heat.

Pour in 2 1/2 cups of water. Bring to a boil. Add the rice and season with salt and pepper. Cover and simmer over low heat for 15 minutes.

Turn into a serving dish. Serve hot.

Creole Risotto

4 servings

1 cup long-grain white rice
2 teaspoons butter
2 cups peeled and diced onions
1/2 cup chopped bacon
1 cup diced tomatoes
2 1/2 cups vegetable broth
1 tablespoon fresh thyme
2 tablespoons chopped parsley
1/2 teaspoon salt
1/4 teaspoon pepper

Soak the rice for 15 minutes and drain.

In a large saucepan, melt the butter. Stir in the onions, bacon, and tomatoes. Brown over low heat. Add the rice. Stir well until transparent.

Pour in the broth, thyme, parsley, salt, and pepper. Bring to a boil and simmer over medium heat for 20 minutes until all the water is absorbed.

Serve hot with Mamie's Chicken with Mushrooms (page 151).

Pumpkin Rice

6 servings

1 teaspoon sunflower oil
1 cup peeled and finely diced pumpkin
1 clove garlic, crushed
1/2 cup peeled and chopped onion
1 tablespoon chopped chives
1/2 cup chopped Canadian bacon
1 cup long-grain white rice
1 teaspoon pepper

Heat the oil in a large saucepan. Stir in the pumpkin, garlic, onion, chives, and bacon. Brown 10 to 15 minutes over medium heat.

Pour in 2 1/2 cups of water. Bring to a boil. Add the rice and pepper. Cover and simmer over low heat for 15 minutes.

Turn into a serving dish.

Serve hot.

Rice and Tomatoes

6 servings

1/4 cup sunflower oil
1 cup chopped tomato
1 clove garlic, crushed
1/2 cup peeled and chopped onion
1 tablespoon chopped chives
1 cup long-grain white rice
1 teaspoon salt
1 teaspoon pepper

Heat the oil in a large saucepan. Stir in the tomato, garlic, onion, and chives. Brown 10 to 15 minutes over medium heat.

Pour in 2 1/2 cups of water. Bring to a boil. Add the rice, salt, and pepper. Cover and simmer over low heat for 15 minutes.

Turn into a serving dish. Serve hot.

Saffron Rice

6 servings

1/4 cup sunflower oil
1 clove garlic, crushed
1/2 cup peeled and chopped onion
1 tablespoon chopped chives
1 can (14 ounces) corn
1 can (14 ounces) sweet peas
1/2 cup chopped Canadian bacon
1 cup long-grain white rice
1 teaspoon saffron
1 teaspoon pepper

Heat the oil in a large saucepan. Stir in the garlic, onion, chives, corn, sweet peas, and bacon. Brown 10 to 15 minutes over medium heat.

Pour in 2 1/2 cups of water. Bring to a boil. Add the rice, saffron, and pepper. Cover and simmer over low heat for 15 minutes until all the water is absorbed.

Turn into a serving dish.

Serve hot.

Red Beans and Rice

4 servings

1 pound red beans
1 teaspoon salt
2 branches thyme
3 tablespoons chopped chives
2 1/2 cups long-grain white rice
1 tablespoon chopped Scotch Bonnet pepper

In a large saucepan combine the red beans with 4 1/2 cups of water. Add salt, thyme, and chives. Bring to a boil and simmer for 40 minutes.

Stir in the rice. Season with Scotch Bonnet pepper. Simmer until all the water is absorbed (10 to 15 minutes).

Serve hot.

Red Beans with Coconut

4 servings

2 cups red beans
1 teaspoon salt
2 branches thyme
3 tablespoons chopped chives
1/2 cup canned coconut milk
1 cup long-grain white rice
1/4 teaspoon Scotch Bonnet pepper

In a large saucepan combine the red beans with 4 cups of water. Add salt, thyme, and chives. Bring to a boil and simmer over medium heat for 30 minutes until most of the water in absorbed.

Stir in the coconut milk and 1 1/2 cups of water. Bring to a boil. Add the rice and simmer for 20 minutes.

Serve hot with red Scotch Bonnet pepper.

Creole Red Beans

4 servings

1 pound red beans
1 teaspoon salt
2 branches thyme
3 tablespoons chopped chives
1 Scotch Bonnet pepper

In a large saucepan combine the red beans with 6 cups of water. Add salt, thyme, and chives. Bring to a boil and simmer over medium heat for 1 hour.

Serve hot with Scotch Bonnet pepper.

Codie's Breadfruit Croquettes

6 servings

4 cups peeled and chopped breadfruit
1/4 cup butter
1 clove garlic, crushed
4 tablespoons chopped parsley
4 tablespoons chopped chives
1 tablespoon salt
1 tablespoon pepper
1 cup flour
4 egg yolks, beaten
1 cup bread crumbs
1/2 cup sunflower oil

Boil the breadfruit in 6 cups of water for 30 minutes until tender. Drain and purée.

In a large bowl, combine the butter, garlic, parsley, chives, salt, and pepper.

Turn the flour, egg yolks, and bread crumbs into 3 separate bowls.

Heat the oil in a frying pan over medium heat.

Prepare the croquettes. Sprinkle a teaspoon of flour on your hands. Roll a tablespoon of breadfruit purée into a cylindrical shape. Dip into the flour, then bread crumbs, and fry. Repeat with the rest of the purée. Once brown, remove and drain the croquettes.

Serve warm.

Breadfruit Fries

6 servings

2 breadfruits
2 cups oil
1 tablespoon salt

Halve, peel, and core the breadfruit. Cut into 1 x 5-inch fries. Wipe with a clean cloth.

Pour the oil in a fritter or a large saucepan and bring to a slight boil over medium heat.

Add about 2 cups of the breadfruit fries and fry for 5 minutes. Drain well and fry again for 5 to 8 minutes until golden. Drain on a paper towel. Repeat with the rest of the breadfruit fries.

Season with salt and serve hot.

Breadfruit Migan

4 servings

1 tablespoon sunflower oil
2 cups diced fatty bacon or cleaned pigtail
1 cup peeled and chopped onion
1/4 cup chopped chives
4 tablespoons chopped parsley
1 teaspoon chopped Scotch Bonnet pepper
4 cups peeled, cored, and chopped breadfruit
1 tablespoon salt
1 tablespoon pepper

Heat the oil in a large saucepan. Add the bacon, onion, chives, parsley, and Scotch Bonnet pepper. Cook for 10 minutes.

Stir in the breadfruit and simmer for 30 minutes. Season with salt and pepper.

Serve hot.

Breadfruit Soufflé

6 servings

2 cups peeled and chopped breadfruit
3 eggs, separated
1/2 cup milk
5 tablespoons butter
1 tablespoon salt
1 teaspoon pepper
1 teaspoon nutmeg

Boil the breadfruit in 4 cups of water for 30 minutes, until tender. Drain and purée.

Preheat oven to 350 degrees F. In a large bowl, combine the breadfruit purée, egg yolks, milk and 4 tablespoons of the butter. Season with salt, pepper, and nutmeg. Stir well.

Grease a soufflé dish or round baking dish with remaining butter. Beat egg whites until stiff peaks form. Fold into the breadfruit mixture.

Turn in the soufflé dish or round baking dish. Bake for 20 to 30 minutes.

Serve at once.

Christmas Pois de Bois

4 servings

1 tablespoon sunflower oil
3 tablespoons chopped chives
2 cloves garlic, crushed
1 tablespoon fresh thyme
2 cups pois de bois or Congo peas
1 teaspoon salt
1 teaspoon pepper
1 cup peeled and chopped malanga (optional)
1 teaspoon brown sugar

Heat the oil in a large saucepan. Stir in the chives, garlic, and thyme. Brown for 3 minutes. Add the pois de bois. Stir well. Season with salt and pepper. Add 1/2 cup of water. Simmer for 5 minutes.

Pour in 6 cups of water. Add the malanga. Simmer over medium heat for 45 minutes until thick and creamy. Add the sugar.

Serve hot with Sandra's Pork Stew (page 148).

Cucumber Court Bouillon

6 servings

2 pounds cucumber, peeled and seeded
2 tablespoons roucou oil
3 cloves garlic, crushed
1 cup sliced tomato
1/2 cup chopped chives
1/2 cup peeled and chopped onion
1/2 cup chopped Canadian bacon
1 teaspoon chopped Scotch Bonnet pepper
1 tablespoon salt
1 tablespoon pepper

Slice the cucumbers lengthwise.

Heat the oil in a large saucepan. Stir in the cucumber, garlic, tomato, chives, onion, and bacon. Brown for 10 to 12 minutes over medium heat.

Add 1/2 cup of water. Season with Scotch Bonnet pepper, salt, and pepper. Simmer 20 to 25 minutes.

Serve hot with Creole Rice (page 75) and Salted Taro (page 104).

Creole Ratatouille

6 servings

1/4 cup sunflower oil
3 cloves garlic, crushed
2 cups peeled and chopped onion
2 tablespoons chopped chives
2 cups peeled and chopped cucumbers
2 cups peeled and chopped eggplants
2 cups peeled and chopped tomatoes
2 cups peeled and chopped pumpkin
1 cup seeded and chopped green peppers
1 cup seeded and chopped red peppers
1 cup seeded and chopped green papaya
1 teaspoon chopped Scotch Bonnet pepper
2 teaspoons fresh thyme
1 bay leaf
2 teaspoons rosemary
1 tablespoon salt
1 tablespoon pepper

Heat the oil over medium heat in a large frying pan. Stir in the garlic, onion, and chives. Cook over medium heat for 5 minutes. Add the cucumbers, eggplants, tomatoes, pumpkin, green and red peppers, and papaya.

Season with Scotch Bonnet pepper, thyme, bay leaf, rosemary, salt, and pepper. Cover and simmer over low heat for 2 1/2 hours.

Serve hot or cold.

Eggplant Cake with Tomato Sauce

6 servings

6 cups sliced eggplants
4 tablespoons salt
3 tablespoons oil
1/2 cup milk
3 eggs
1 teaspoon pepper

Tomato Sauce:

2 tablespoons oil
1/2 cup peeled and chopped onion
1 clove garlic, crushed
1 can (28 ounces) crushed tomatoes
1 teaspoon tomato paste
1 cup chicken or vegetable broth
2 teaspoons chopped basil
1 teaspoon salt
1 teaspoon pepper

Salt the eggplants in a colander for 30 minutes. Wipe with paper towels.

Heat 2 tablespoons of the oil in a large saucepan and stir in the eggplants. Cover and cook over medium heat for 30 minutes. Drain and purée in a blender or sieve.

Preheat oven to 300 degrees F. In a bowl combine the eggplant purée with the milk, eggs, and pepper. Stir until smooth and creamy.

Grease a cake pan with the remaining oil and turn in the eggplant purée. Place the pan in a large shallow baking dish halfway filled with water. Place both dishes in the oven and bake for 40 minutes.

Prepare the tomato sauce. In a saucepan, heat the oil and add the onions and garlic. Cook over low heat for 10 minutes. Add the crushed tomatoes, tomato paste, chicken broth, basil, salt, and pepper. Simmer for 45 minutes.

Once cooled, turn out the eggplant cake onto a serving plate. Coat with tomato sauce. Serve warm.

Eggplant Gratin

6 servings

3 eggplants, peeled and halved
1 slice bread
1/4 cup milk
1 clove garlic, crushed
1 cup peeled and chopped onion
1 teaspoon salt
1 teaspoon pepper
1/2 cup bread crumbs
1 tablespoon butter

Combine the eggplant with a 1/4 cup of water in a shallow dish. Microwave on high power for 30 minutes. Preheat the oven to 350 degrees F.

In a small bowl, combine the bread with milk. Soak for 10 minutes. Drain.

Drain the eggplants and purée. Stir in the garlic, onion, soaked bread, salt, and pepper. Mix well.

Turn into a baking dish. Sprinkle with bread crumbs and dots of butter. Bake for 20 minutes.

Serve hot.

Eggplant Purée

4 servings

4 cups peeled and diced eggplants
4 tablespoons salt
4 tablespoons butter
1 clove garlic, crushed
2 tablespoons chopped parsley
1 teaspoon red Scotch Bonnet pepper (optional)

In a colander salt the eggplants for 30 minutes. Wipe them thoroughly with paper towels.

Heat 2 tablespoons of butter in a pan. Add the eggplant and cook for 30 minutes over low heat. Transfer to a blender or a food processor and process until puréed.

Heat the puree over low heat for 10 minutes with the remaining 2 tablespoons of butter, the garlic, parsley, and Scotch Bonnet pepper.

Serve hot with Lamb Roast (page 143) or Roast Pork (page 147).

Baked Eggplant

6 servings

3 eggplants, diced
1 teaspoon salt
1 teaspoon pepper
1 clove garlic, crushed
2 tablespoons chives
1 teaspoon chopped Scotch Bonnet pepper (optional)
1 teaspoon oil
1/2 cup chopped Canadian bacon
1 cup grated Swiss or Gruyère cheese

Bring 4 cups of water to a boil. Stir in the eggplants, salt, pepper, garlic, chives, and Scotch Bonnet pepper. Bring to a boil and simmer for 45 minutes. Drain. Preheat the oven to 300 degrees F.

Heat the oil in a frying pan. Brown the bacon for 5 to 8 minutes over medium heat. Stir in the eggplants. Stir well.

Turn into a baking dish. Sprinkle with grated cheese.
Bake for 20 minutes.

Serve hot.

Lolo's Stuffed Eggplant

6 servings

3 eggplants, cleaned and halved lengthwise
6 tablespoons salt
2 slices white bread
1/2 cup milk
2 tablespoons sunflower oil
4 tablespoons chopped chives
1/4 cup thinly sliced bacon
1 clove garlic, crushed
3 tablespoons chopped parsley
1 tablespoon pepper
1/2 teaspoon chopped red Scotch Bonnet pepper
6 tablespoons bread crumbs
6 tablespoons grated Swiss or Gruyère cheese
3 teaspoons butter

With a sharp knife, notch the eggplant's flesh. Salt the eggplants in a colander for 30 minutes.

Preheat the oven to 350 degrees F. Soak the bread in milk.

In a large frying pan, heat the oil over medium heat and add the eggplant face down. Cook for 15 minutes until the flesh becomes tender.

With a spoon, carefully remove the eggplant's flesh without damaging the skin. In a large bowl mix the flesh with chives, bacon, garlic, parsley, pepper, Scotch Bonnet pepper, and drained bread.

Fill each eggplant's skin with the stuffing and top with 1 tablespoon bread crumbs, 1 tablespoon of grated cheese, and 1/2 teaspoon butter. Bake for 20 minutes.

Serve hot with Creole Rice (page 75).

Giraumonade

4 servings

4 cups peeled and diced giraumon (Chinese pumpkin)
1/4 cup sunflower oil
1/4 cup chopped chives
1 clove garlic, crushed
2 tablespoons chopped parsley
2 tablespoons fresh thyme
1 tablespoon chopped basil
1 teaspoon salt
1 teaspoon pepper
1 teaspoon chopped Scotch Bonnet pepper
2 teaspoons butter
1/4 cup bread crumbs
1/4 cup grated Swiss or Gruyère cheese

Bring 4 cup of water to a boil. Add the pumpkin and simmer for 30 minutes. Drain and puree.

Preheat oven to 300 degrees F. Heat the oil in a saucepan. Stir in the chives, garlic, parsley, thyme, and basil. Simmer for 10 minutes over medium heat.

Pour in the pumpkin puree. Season with salt, pepper, and Scotch Bonnet pepper. Stir well and cook for another 5 minutes.

Turn in a shallow oven dish. Sprinkle with dots of butter, bread crumbs, and grated cheese.

Bake for 15 minutes.

Serve hot.

Lentil and Dombrés

6 servings

1 cup flour
1 1/2 tablespoons salt
2 cups lentils
2 tablespoons chopped parsley
2 tablespoons chopped chives
1 clove garlic, crushed
1 teaspoon pepper
1 cup chopped bacon

Combine the flour, salt, and 1/4 cup of water. Knead well until smooth and elastic. Add flour if necessary. Roll into a ball and let rest for 1 hour.

In a large saucepan combine the lentils, with 4 cups of water. Bring to a boil and simmer over medium heat for 15 minutes.

Prepare the dombrés. Flour your hands and roll the dough into small balls of 2 inches in diameter.

Add 1 cup of water to the lentils. Stir in the dombrés, parsley, chives, garlic, pepper, and bacon. Bring to a boil and simmer for 20 minutes. Turn into a serving dish.

Serve hot.

Mamie's Yellow Bananas

6 servings

2 pounds ripe (yellow) plantain
1 tablespoon oil
2 teaspoons salt

Peel and cut the plantains in half with a sharp knife.

In a large saucepan combine 8 cups of water, oil, and salt. Bring to a boil and simmer for 25 minutes until tender. Drain.

Serve hot with a meat, fish, or chicken dish.

Papaya Gratin

6 servings

1 pound green papaya, peeled, seeded, and diced
1 tablespoon salt
1 teaspoon chopped Scotch Bonnet pepper
3 tablespoons chopped chives
2 tablespoons chopped sorrel
4 tablespoons butter
6 tablespoons flour
2 cups milk
1 cup grated Swiss or Gruyère cheese

In a large saucepan combine the green papaya, salt, Scotch Bonnet pepper, chives, sorrel, and 4 cups water. Bring to a boil and simmer 30 minutes over medium heat. Drain.

Preheat the oven to 300 degrees F. Prepare the béchamel sauce. Melt 3 tablespoons of the butter in a saucepan. Stir in the flour and milk. Simmer over low heat stirring constantly until thick and creamy. Turn off the heat and stir in the papaya.

Pour in a shallow baking dish. Sprinkle with grated cheese and the remaining 1 tablespoon of butter. Bake for 45 minutes.

Serve hot.

Papaya Soufflé

6 servings

2 cups peeled, seeded, and chopped green papaya
2 tablespoons salt
2 tablespoons chopped chives
2 tablespoons chopped sorrel
1 teaspoon chopped Scotch Bonnet pepper
3 eggs, separated
1/2 cup milk
1/2 cup butter
1/4 cup grated Swiss or Gruyère cheese
1 teaspoon pepper

In a large saucepan, combine the papaya, 1 tablespoon of the salt, the chives, sorrel, and Scotch Bonnet pepper. Bring to a boil and simmer for 30 minutes, until tender. Drain and puree. Drain again.

In a large bowl, combine the papaya puree, egg yolks, milk, 1/4 cup of the butter, and cheese. Season with remaining 1 teaspoon of salt and pepper.

Beat the egg whites until stiff peaks form. Fold the egg whites into the papaya mixture. Turn in a greased soufflé dish or round baking dish. Sprinkle with the remaining 1/4 cup butter, cut into pieces.

Bake for 20 to 30 minutes.

Serve at once.

Sandra's Plantain Delice

6 servings

6 tablespoons butter
2 cups chopped ham
3 tablespoons chopped chives
1/2 cup peeled and chopped onion
1 clove garlic, crushed
2 tablespoons chopped parsley
6 cups peeled and chopped ripe plantains
6 tablespoons flour
2 cups milk
1 cup grated Swiss or Gruyère cheese

Heat 1 tablespoon of the butter in a frying pan over medium heat. Stir in the ham, chives, onion, garlic, and parsley and cook for 10 minutes. Preheat oven to 350 degrees F.

In a second frying pan combine the plantain with 1 tablespoon of the butter. Cook over low heat for 20 minutes until the plantains are tender.

Prepare a béchamel sauce. In a small saucepan, melt the remaining 3 tablespoons of butter over low heat. Stir in the flour until creamy. Add the milk and stir constantly until obtaining a thick cream.

Combine the ham and plantain in a shallow baking dish. Pour in the béchamel sauce. Sprinkle with grated cheese.

Bake for 30 minutes.

Serve hot with Lamb Roast (page 143) or Roast Pork (page 147).

Plantain Gratin

6 servings

4 tablespoons butter
8 ripe plantains, halved
6 tablespoons flour
2 cups milk
3 tablespoons chopped chives
1 teaspoon nutmeg
2 teaspoons salt
1 teaspoon pepper
1 cup grated Swiss or Gruyère cheese
1 cup bread crumbs

Preheat oven to 350 degrees F. Grease a shallow baking dish with 1 tablespoon of the butter. Turn in the plantains.

Prepare the béchamel sauce. Melt the remaining 3 tablespoons butter in a saucepan. Stir in the flour and milk, chives, nutmeg, salt, and pepper. Simmer over low heat, stirring constantly, for 15 minutes until thick and creamy. Pour onto the plantains.

Sprinkle with grated cheese and bread crumbs. Bake for 45 minutes.

Serve hot with Duck Flambé (page 154).

Plantain Fries

6 servings

2 pounds ripe (yellow) plantains
2 cups oil
1 tablespoon salt

Peel the plantains and slice them in 1-inch slices. Wipe with a clean cloth.

Pour the oil in a fritter or a large saucepan and bring to a slight boil over medium heat. Add about 2 cups of plantain and fry for 8 to 10 minutes. Drain in a colander lined with paper towel. Repeat with the rest of the plantain.

Season with salt and serve hot.

Salted Taro

6 servings

2 pounds taro (*igname*), peeled
1 lime
1 tablespoon sunflower oil
1 tablespoon salt

Cut the taro into large pieces. Rinse under tap water.

Combine 8 cups of water, squeezed lime juice, oil, and salt in a large saucepan. Stir in the taro. Bring to a boil and simmer for 25 to 30 minutes until tender. Drain.

Serve hot with fish or meat dish.

Taro Fries

6 servings

2 1/2 pounds taro (*igname*)
2 cups oil
1 tablespoons salt

Peel the taro. Cut them in 1 x 4-inch fries. Wipe with a clean cloth.

Pour the oil in a fritter or a large saucepan and bring to a slight boil over medium heat.

Add half of the taro and fry for 10 minutes. Drain on a paper towel. Repeat with the other half.

Season with salt and serve hot.

Salted Sweet Potatoes

6 servings

2 pounds sweet potatoes
1 tablespoon sunflower oil
2 teaspoons salt

Combine 8 cups of water, sweet potatoes, oil, and salt in a large saucepan.

Bring to a boil and simmer for 25 to 30 minutes until tender. Drain.

Peel and serve hot with Court Bouillon Saintois (page 121) or Fish Blaff (page 122).

Sweet Potato Fries

6 servings

2 pounds sweet potatoes
2 cups oil
1 tablespoon salt

Clean and peel the sweet potatoes. Cut them into 1-inch fries. Wipe with a clean cloth.

Pour the oil in a fritter or a large saucepan and bring to a slight boil over medium heat.

Add about 2 cups of the sweet potatoes and fry for 5 minutes. Drain well and fry again for 5 minutes. Drain on a paper towel. Repeat with the rest of the sweet potatoes.

Season with salt and serve hot.

Spinach à la Béchamel

6 servings

4 to 5 pounds fresh spinach
1/2 cup diced chives
1 tablespoon dried thyme
3 bay leaves
1/2 cup chopped parsley
Béchamel Sauce with Onions (page 193)
3 hard-boiled eggs, peeled and sliced
1 cup peeled and diced tomato
1 tablespoon salt

Wash and drain the spinach. Bring 4 cups of salted water to a boil. Add chives, thyme, bay leaves, parsley, and spinach. Cook for 15 minutes.

Drain spinach and herbs. Purée in blender. Set aside.

Prepare the béchamel sauce with onions. Add the spinach and let it simmer for 10 minutes. Turn onto a serving dish.

Garnish the hot spinach with the eggs and tomato slices. Season with salt.

Serve warm.

Stuffed Christophenes

6 servings

6 christophenes (2 to 3 pounds)
1/2 pound stale bread
3 tablespoons oil
1/2 pound ground pork or ham
1 clove garlic, crushed
1 cup peeled and diced onion
1/4 cup diced chives
1 tablespoon dried thyme
1/4 cup chopped parsley plus additional for garnish
1 tablespoon salt
1 tablespoon pepper
3 tablespoons butter
2 cups bread crumbs

Preheat oven to 400 degrees F.

Wash the christophenes and cook them in salted water for 12 minutes. Let them cool and cut them in half. Remove the cores and scoop out the flesh carefully with a spoon, without damaging the skins. Reserve the skins.

Soak the stale bread in water for 5 minutes. Drain and squeeze between palms to remove excess water. Mix the bread and christophenes together.

In a saucepan heat the oil and add the pork, garlic, onion, chives, thyme, parsley, salt, and pepper. Cook for 5 minutes. Add the mashed christophenes, cook for another 5 minutes.

Fill the christophene skins with the stuffing, placing a knob of butter and some bread crumbs on the top. Place them on a baking sheet.

Bake for 15 minutes, garnish with parsley, and serve hot with Roast Pork (page 147).

Fish and Shellfish

Parrot fish—a name that immediately transports you to a paradise island. I remember snorkeling as a kid around the *Ilet Pigeon* not far from Basse-Terre in Guadeloupe. This small island is a natural reserve created by the celebrated Captain Jacques Cousteau. The colors and patterns of the seascape are still vivid in my memory; it was just like swimming in a *tableau vivant*. The produce of the sea is so fresh that it tastes best just grilled or dressed with savory sauces like the spicy *Sauce Chien*. The national dish, the *Fish Court Bouillon* with its clear tomato broth, is a delightful and easy way of cooking any type of medium-size fish.

Among the shellfish, my favorite are the *palourdes* or large clams. My father cooks them in a mix of lime, chives, spices and a drop of pimiento that adds an unexpected flavor to the flesh. The *langouste* or tropical lobster is becoming a rare delicacy in the French Caribbean islands. When simply grilled, the flesh keeps its fluffiness and delicate flavor. I usually add a few drops of *Sauce Chien* or spicy mayonnaise and eat it with Creole rice. Another traditional fish is the salted codfish. Although imported, it has become a common ingredient over the years. Prepared in *Chiquetaille*, it can be refrigerated for 4 days and added to any vegetable or rice dish.

Fish and Shellfish

Codfish and Rice

Alain's Poyo and Codfish

Codfish Brandade

Codfish au Gratin

Creole Codfish

Crayfish Blaff

Fish Court Bouillon

Fish Blaff

Fish Cake Hoff Fala

Fried Fish

Grilled Lobsters

Grilled Tuna

Jack's Clams

Lobster Fricassée

Octopus Fricassée

Shrimp with Coconut

Steamed Fish à la Jacques

Stuffed Clams

Swordfish Blaff

Marinated Grilled Swordfish

Tuna Tartar

Vivaneau au Roucou

Codfish and Rice

4 servings

1 pound salted codfish
1/4 cup sunflower oil
3 cups chopped tomatoes
1/2 cup chopped chives
4 tablespoons chopped parsley
1 clove garlic, crushed
2 tablespoons fresh thyme
1 Scotch Bonnet pepper
1 tablespoon roucou (optional)
1 cup long-grain white rice

Soak the codfish in cold water for 3 hours, then drain. In a large saucepan bring 4 cups of water to a boil. Stir in the codfish. Boil for 10 minutes. Drain. Repeat and let cool. Skin, bone and crumble the flesh.

In a large saucepan, heat the oil over medium heat. Stir in the tomatoes, chives, parsley, garlic, and thyme. Brown for 5 minutes. Add the fish and brown for 10 minutes.

Stir in 2 cups of water, the Scotch Bonnet pepper, and roucou. Bring to a boil.

Add the rice, cover, and simmer for 20 minutes. Lower the heat, uncover, and simmer until all the water is absorbed (10 to 15 minutes).

Serve hot.

Alain's Poyo and Codfish

4 servings

1 pound piece salted codfish
1 tablespoon salt
1/4 cup sunflower oil
1 pound taro, peeled and halved
8 poyos, peeled
1 cup peeled and sliced onion

Soak the codfish in cold water for 3 hours. Drain.

In a large saucepan bring 4 cups of water to a boil. Stir in the codfish and boil for 45 minutes.

In a large saucepan, combine 4 cups of water, salt, and 2 tablespoons of the oil. Bring to a boil. Add the taro and simmer for 20 minutes. Add the poyos. Bring to a boil and cook for another 20 to 30 minutes.

Drain the codfish and let cool. Bone and skin and cut into pieces.

Heat the remaining 2 tablespoons of oil in a frying pan over high heat. Drop in the codfish and cover. Fry 8 to 10 minutes on each side. Set aside on a serving dish.

Brown the onion in the same pan, stirring constantly. Turn onto the codfish.

Drain the poyos and taro. Turn into a serving dish.

Serve hot.

Codfish Brandade

6 servings

1 pound salted codfish
1 1/2 pounds potatoes (about 5), peeled and diced
3 tablespoons oil
2 tablespoons butter
1 tablespoon chopped parsley
2 tablespoons chopped chives
1 cup peeled and sliced onion
1 clove garlic, crushed
1 teaspoon salt
1 teaspoon pepper
2 cups milk
1 cup grated Swiss or Gruyère cheese

Soak the codfish overnight in 8 cups of water. Drain.

In a large saucepan, combine the potatoes and codfish. Cover with water. Bring to a boil and simmer for 25 minutes until tender. Drain. Bone and skin the codfish. Purée the potatoes and codfish.

Preheat the oven to 350 degrees F.

Heat the oil and butter in a saucepan. Stir in the parsley, chives, onion, garlic, salt, and pepper. Cook over medium heat for 5 to 7 minutes. Stir in the potatoes and codfish purée. Pour in the milk. Stir well until smooth. Cook for 5 minutes.

Turn into a greased glass baking dish. Sprinkle with cheese.
Bake for 10 to 15 minutes.

Serve hot with a mixed green salad.

Codfish au Gratin

6 servings

1 1/2 pounds salted codfish
1 cup white wine vinegar
3 tablespoons oil
1 1/2 pounds potatoes (about 5), peeled and diced
2 tablespoons butter
1 cup peeled and diced onion
1 clove garlic, crushed
1/2 cup chopped parsley
1 tablespoon dried thyme
1 teaspoon pepper
1 cup grated Gruyère or Swiss cheese
1 cup bread crumbs

Preheat oven to 350 degrees F.

Soak the fish for 3 hours in vinegar combined with 4 cups of water. Drain.

In a pan heat the oil. Add the fish and potatoes. Cook for 30 minutes then purée in a blender.

In a saucepan melt the butter. Add onion, garlic, parsley, thyme, and pepper. Add the codfish and potatoes mixture.

Pour the mixture into a greased pie dish and sprinkle with grated cheese and bread crumbs on top.

Bake for 10 minutes until browned.

Creole Codfish

6 servings

1/2 pound salted codfish
1 cup sunflower oil
1 cup peeled and chopped onion
2 tablespoons white wine vinegar
2 tablespoons chopped chives
1 tablespoon peeled and crushed garlic
1 tablespoon chopped parsley

In a large saucepan bring 2 cups of water to a boil. Add the codfish and cook for 15 to 20 minutes over medium heat. Drain and let it cool.

In glass jar, combine the oil, onion, vinegar, chives, garlic, and parsley.

Prepare the codfish. Remove the bones and skin and crumble the flesh. Add to the jar and close. Let the fish marinate for at least 1 day before serving.

Serve with salted breadfruit, taro, or plantain.

Crayfish Blaff

6 servings

1 cup peeled and sliced onion
1/2 cup chopped parsley
2 tablespoons fresh thyme
1 bay leaf
3 chives, chopped
4 cloves garlic, peeled and crushed
1 teaspoon salt
1/2 teaspoon pepper
24 crayfish
2 tablespoons freshly squeezed lime juice
1 teaspoon chopped Scotch Bonnet pepper

In a large saucepan, combine 4 cups of water with onion, parsley, thyme, bay leaf, chives, 2 of the garlic cloves, salt, and pepper. Bring to a boil and add the crayfish. Simmer for 5 minutes. Drain.

In a bowl, combine the lime juice with the remaining 2 garlic cloves.

Turn the crayfish onto a serving dish. Serve warm with the lime and Scotch Bonnet pepper on the side.

Fish Court Bouillon

6 servings

2 pounds vivaneau, or other white fish
3 cloves garlic, crushed
1 teaspoon chopped Scotch Bonnet pepper
1 tablespoon salt
1 tablespoon pepper
1/2 cup freshly squeezed lime juice
2 tablespoons roucou or sunflower oil
1/2 cup chopped chives
1/2 cup peeled and chopped onion
2 cups chopped tomatoes
1 lime, halved
1 clove garlic, peeled
1 chive, halved

Clean and bone the fish.

Prepare a marinade. In a large shallow dish combine crushed garlic, Scotch Bonnet pepper, salt, pepper, and lime juice. Soak the fish for 2 to 3 hours. Drain.

In a large saucepan heat the oil over low heat. Stir in the chopped chives and onion. Cook for 10 to 15 minutes stirring regularly. Add tomatoes and simmer an additional 10 minutes over medium heat.

Stir in the fish and add 1 to 1 1/2 cups of water (the water should barely cover the fish). Simmer 15 minutes. Turn off the heat.

Squeeze the halved lime over the fish. Stir in the garlic clove and chive.

Serve hot with Creole Rice (page 75).

Variation or Court Bouillon Saintois:
Omit the tomatoes.

Fish Blaff

6 servings

3 to 4 pounds tuna or swordfish, sliced
1 lime, halved
1 teaspoon salt
1 teaspoon pepper
1 clove garlic, minced
1/2 teaspoon chopped Scotch Bonnet pepper
4 tablespoons freshly squeezed lime juice
1/2 cup chopped chives
2 tablespoons dry thyme
1/2 cup chopped parsley
3 tablespoons oil

Clean and bone the fish. Rub with lime halves.

Prepare a marinade. Combine 1 cup of water, salt, pepper, garlic, Scotch Bonnet pepper, and 2 tablespoons of the lime juice. Add the fish. Let it soak for 2 hours.

In a fish kettle combine 4 cups of water with chives, thyme, and parsley. Bring to a boil for 15 minutes. Add the fish to the boiling water and cook for 10 minutes. Turn off the heat. Cover and let poach for 20 minutes.

Add the remaining 2 tablespoons of lime juice and the oil. Let it cool a few minutes before serving with root vegetables.

Fish Cake Hoff Fala

6 servings

4 tablespoons chopped chives
2 tablespoons chopped parsley
2 tablespoons fresh thyme
1/2 teaspoon chopped Scotch Bonnet pepper
4 pounds swordfish
1/4 cup sunflower oil
1 cup stale bread
3 eggs
1 cup milk powder
1 Short Crust Pastry (page 161)
2 cups Béchamel Sauce with Eggs (page 192)

In a large saucepan, combine 4 cups of water, chives, parsley, thyme, and Scotch Bonnet pepper. Add the fish. Bring to a boil and simmer for 20 minutes. Drain the fish. Skin, bone, and purée.

Preheat the oven to 350 degrees F.

Heat the oil in a saucepan over medium heat. Stir in the bread, eggs, milk powder, and fish. Brown for 10 minutes over low heat.

Line a 10-inch diameter greased cake pan with the short crust pastry. Turn in the fish.

Pour the Béchamel over the fish. Bake for 45 minutes.

Turn over a serving dish. Serve warm.

Fried Fish

4 servings

1 pound fish (bonito, swordfish, mahi-mahi)
1/4 cup freshly squeezed lime juice
1 clove garlic, crushed
1 teaspoon pepper
1/4 cup sunflower oil
1 cup peeled and thinly sliced onion

Clean and bone the fish. Season with lime juice, garlic, and pepper.

Heat the oil in a frying pan. Brown the fish over medium heat, 5 to 10 minutes on each side. Turn in a serving dish.

Fry the onions in the same pan, stirring constantly for 5 minutes. Arrange on top of the fish.

Serve hot with salted vegetables

Grilled Lobsters

2 servings

2 limes, squeezed
2 tablespoons sunflower oil
2 lobsters, halved
1 teaspoon salt
1/2 teaspoon pepper
1 cup Sauce Chien (page 194)

Preheat the grill.

In a small bowl mix the lime juice with oil. Pour over the lobster flesh. Season with salt and pepper.

Place on the grill, face down. Grill for 5 to 8 minutes then turn and grill for another 8 minutes.

Serve with Sauce Chien (page 194) or Spicy Mayonnaise (page 195) and vegetable gratin.

Grilled Tuna

6 servings

2 cloves garlic, peeled and crushed
1/2 cup chopped parsley
2 tablespoons fresh thyme
3 chives, chopped
1 cup peeled and diced onion
2 shallots, peeled and chopped
2 tablespoons freshly squeezed lime juice
1 teaspoon salt
1/2 teaspoon pepper
1/4 teaspoon crushed cloves
1/2 teaspoon chopped Scotch Bonnet pepper
2 pounds fresh tuna fish, cleaned and sliced
1 tablespoon butter
1 tablespoon oil
1 lime, sliced

Prepare the marinade in a large bowl. Combine garlic, parsley, thyme, chives, onion, shallots, lime juice, salt, pepper, cloves, and Scotch Bonnet pepper. Rub the fish with butter and soak in marinade for 1 1/2 hours in the refrigerator.

Preheat the oven to 250 degrees F.

Grease a baking dish with oil. Add the fish and bake for 30 minutes on each side. Baste regularly with marinade.

Serve very hot with Scotch Bonnet pepper and lime on the side.

Jack's Clams

6 servings

24 medium-size clams, cleaned and brushed
4 tablespoons chopped chives
2 tablespoons fresh thyme
4 tablespoons chopped parsley
1 lime, halved
1 teaspoon crushed garlic
1 chopped red Scotch Bonnet pepper (optional)

In a large saucepan combine the clams with 3 tablespoons of the chives, thyme, and parsley. Cover and cook over medium heat until the clams are wide opened. Turn off the heat.

Squeeze the halved lime over the clams. Stir in the garlic and remaining chives. Add the Scotch Bonnet pepper.

Serve hot.

Lobster Fricassée

6 servings

4 pounds lobsters
2 cups oil
1 cup peeled and sliced onion
3 cups diced tomatoes
1 tablespoon chopped chives
1 tablespoon dried thyme
1/2 glass white wine
3 cloves garlic, crushed
1/2 cup chopped parsley
2 tablespoons freshly squeezed lime juice

Wash and brush the lobsters well. Cut them in 8 pieces with shell and roll them in the flour. Brown in 1/2 cup of hot oil. Drain.

In a frying pan, combine 2 tablespoons of oil, onions, tomatoes, chives, and thyme. Simmer for 15 minutes.

Add the lobsters, white wine, and 3 cups of water. Cook for 15 minutes. Add the garlic, parsley, and lime juice.

Serve at once with rice.

Octopus Fricassée

6 servings

2 pounds small octopus
1 lime, halved
2 tablespoons sunflower oil
1 tablespoon fresh thyme
2 tablespoons chopped parsley
1 clove garlic, crushed
2 bay leaves
4 tablespoons chopped chives
1/2 teaspoon crushed cloves
4 tablespoons freshly squeezed lime juice

Clean the octopus. Remove and discard the intestines, ink sack, eyes, and beak. Wash it thoroughly under tap water and cut into pieces. Rub with halved lime.

Bring 4 cups of water to a boil. Stir in the octopus and simmer for 30 to 45 minutes. Reserve 1/2 cup of cooking water. Drain the octopus and rub with a clean cloth to remove the skin and tentacles.

Heat the oil in the large saucepan. Stir in the thyme, parsley, garlic, bay leaves, chives, and cloves. Brown over medium heat for 5 minutes.

Add the octopus and the cooking water. Simmer 20 minutes. Stir occasionally.

Sprinkle with lime juice. Turn into a serving dish.

Serve hot with Red Beans and Rice (page 81).

# Shrimp with Coconut

4 servings

2 tablespoons olive oil
1/2 cup peeled and chopped onion
1 clove garlic, crushed
3 cups chopped tomatoes
1/2 cup dry white wine
1 tablespoon fresh thyme
2 bay leaves
1 teaspoon chopped Scotch Bonnet pepper
1 tablespoon salt
1 teaspoon pepper
1 can (14 ounces) coconut milk
1 pound jumbo shrimp shelled
1/4 cup grated coconut

Heat the oil in a deep frying pan. Add the onion and garlic. Cook over medium heat for 10 minutes. Stir in the tomatoes, white wine, thyme, and bay leaves. Season with Scotch Bonnet pepper, salt, and pepper. Simmer for 10 minutes. Add the coconut milk and simmer for another 10 minutes.

Stir in the shrimp and sprinkle with grated coconut. Cook for 10 minutes.

Serve hot with Creole Rice (page 75).

Steamed Fish à la Jacques

6 servings

One 2 to 3 pound red snapper
1/2 cup freshly squeezed lime juice
3 cloves garlic, crushed
1/4 cup chopped chives
1 tablespoon salt
1 tablespoon pepper
1 tablespoon dried rosemary
2 tablespoons dried thyme
1 tablespoon dried oregano
1 red Scotch Bonnet pepper

Clean and bone the fish carefully. Combine the lime juice, garlic, chives, salt, and pepper in a large shallow dish. Marinate the fish in the refrigerator for 4 to 5 hours. Drain.

Fill the 1/2 of the lower part of a steamer with water. Add the rosemary, thyme, and oregano.

Steam the fish for 30 to 40 minutes until tender. Prick with a sharp knife to check on cooking.

Turn in a serving dish. Insert the red Scotch Bonnet pepper in the fish's mouth and serve at once.

Serve hot.

Swordfish Blaff

6 servings

2 pounds swordfish, sliced
5 limes, halved
1 cup white wine
1 tablespoon oil
3 cloves
1 tablespoon allspice
2 tablespoons chopped chives
2 cloves garlic, crushed
1 teaspoon pepper
1 cup peeled and sliced onion
2 tablespoons chopped parsley
1 teaspoon chopped Scotch Bonnet pepper

Clean and bone the fish. Season with juice of 1 lime.

In a large saucepan, combine 1 cup of water and wine. Stir in juice of 3 limes, oil, cloves, allspice, chives, garlic, pepper, onion, parsley, and Scotch Bonnet pepper. Bring to a boil over medium heat.

Stir in the fish and boil 10 to 15 minutes. Turn off the heat and sprinkle with juice of 1 lime. Turn into a shallow serving dish. Cover with the cooked onions, parsley, and sauce.

Serve hot with salted root vegetables.

Marinated Grilled Swordfish

6 servings

2 tablespoons freshly squeezed lime juice
1 teaspoon salt
1/2 teaspoon chopped Scotch Bonnet pepper
2 cloves garlic, crushed
5 chopped chives
1/2 cup chopped parsley
2 tablespoons fresh thyme
1 teaspoon allspice
1/2 teaspoon pepper
2 pounds fresh swordfish, sliced
2 tablespoons flour
4 tablespoons oil
1 cup peeled and sliced onion

Prepare the marinade. In a large shallow dish combine the lime juice, salt, Scotch Bonnet pepper, garlic, chives, parsley, thyme, allspice, and pepper. Add the fish and cover with water. Soak for 1 1/2 hours. Turn the fish regularly.

Sift the flour onto a large flat plate. Dry each slice of fish with paper towels and coat with flour.

Heat oil in a large frying pan over high heat. Fry the fish 4 minutes on each side until golden. Drain on paper towels to remove oil excess. Turn onto a serving plate.

In the same pan, fry the onion slices for 2 to 3 minutes. Drain and serve with the fish.

Tuna Tartar

4 servings

2 pounds fresh tuna, sliced
3/4 cup fresh squeezed lime juice
1/4 cup peeled and chopped shallots
1/4 cup chopped parsley
1/4 cup chopped chives
1 Scotch Bonnet pepper, chopped
1 tablespoon olive oil
1 teaspoon salt
1 teaspoon pepper

Skin and bone the tuna. Crumble the flesh into tiny pieces. Turn in a shallow dish. Add lime juice, shallots, parsley, chives, Scotch Bonnet pepper, olive oil, salt, and pepper. Stir well. Refrigerate for 2 to 3 hours.

Turn into a serving dish and serve at once.

Vivaneau au Roucou

6 servings

2 pounds vivaneau or red snapper
1 teaspoon salt
1/2 teaspoon pepper
4 cloves garlic, peeled and crushed
2 tablespoons roucou
3 chives, chopped
1/2 cup chopped parsley
1 tablespoon red butter or regular butter
2 tablespoons freshly squeezed lime juice

Rub the fish with salt, pepper, and 2 of the crushed garlic cloves. Marinate for 1 hour.

In a large saucepan, melt the roucou over low heat. Add the chives, parsley, and red butter. Brown 3 to 4 minutes. Add the fish and 1/2 cup of water. Simmer for 8 minutes.

Add the lime juice and the remaining 2 crushed garlic cloves.

Turn onto a serving dish. Serve hot with Creole Rice (page 75).

Meat and Poultry

Both Guadeloupe and Martinique are volcanic islands, and green pastures make up an important part of the terrain. Although most of the beef is imported from France, local cattle and poultry offer tasty and tender pieces. Pork and lamb prepared in spicy stews or curries called "Colombo" are among the classics of French Caribbean cuisine. Variety meats such as tripes or pigtails are also much appreciated. Inherited from the African culinary tradition, the *Bébélé* is a national dish prepared with tripes and various vegetables.

For Christmas, the traditional dinner includes, among other delicacies, pork stew with *pois-de-bois* and ham. My grandfather, a fine cook and gourmet, prepared every year the *Jambon de Noël*, glazed in brown sugar and trimmed with pineapple slices. I remember sneaking in the family kitchen the day before Christmas to help him prick the big ham with cloves and arrange the pineapple slices. My Aunt Codie carried on the tradition of the *Jambon de Noël* and she serves it with a delicious parsley butter and fresh bread.

Marinated in lime, garlic and spices, poultry is cooked in fricassée, Colombo, or just grilled. Chicken prepared with mushrooms and accompanied with Creole Rice is one of my favorite dishes.

Meat and Poultry

Bébélé

Beef or Lamb Stew

Lamb Roast

Roast Leg of Lamb

Lentils and Bacon

Pork Colombo

Roast Pork

Sandra's Pork Stew

Coconut Chicken

Chicken Colombo

Mamie's Chicken with Mushrooms

Lina's Chicken Fricassée

Daddy's Pineapple Ham

Duck Flambé

Turkey Wing Stew

Bébélé

6 servings

2 pounds beef tripe
8 tablespoons freshly squeezed lime juice
2 teaspoons salt
20 Dombrés (page 200)
1 cup peeled and chopped breadfruit
8 plantains, peeled and diced
1 tablespoon chopped chives
1/2 cup chopped parsley
1 tablespoon dried thyme
3 cloves garlic, crushed
1 teaspoon pepper
1 teaspoon chopped Scotch Bonnet pepper

Clean the tripe under tap water. Rub with 7 tablespoons lime juice. Cut into small pieces. Combine with 6 cups of water and the salt in a large saucepan or a pressure cooker. Cover. Bring to a boil over medium heat and simmer for 30 minutes.

Prepare the dough and form the dombrés. Add the breadfruit and bananas to the tripe. Cover with water and cook for another 30 minutes.

Add the dombrés, chives, parsley, thyme, garlic, pepper, and Scotch Bonnet pepper. Stir well. Cook for another 10 minutes. Season with salt and remaining 1 tablespoon lime juice. Serve hot.

Beef or Lamb Stew

4 servings

1 pound beef flank or lamb, cut into pieces
1 cup peeled and chopped onion
1 clove garlic, crushed
1 tablespoon white wine vinegar
1 teaspoon salt
1 teaspoon pepper
1/4 cup sunflower oil
2 carrots, peeled

Clean the meat under cold tap water. Drain and wipe. Combine with onion, garlic, vinegar, salt and pepper in a shallow dish. Cover and refrigerate for 30 minutes.

Heat the oil in a large saucepan. Brown the meat and seasonings for 5 to 10 minutes. Stir in 1/2 cup of water and the carrots. Simmer for 20 minutes.

Serve hot with Red Beans and Rice (page 81).

Lamb Roast

4 servings

1 1/2-pound lamb roast
1 tablespoon white wine vinegar
1 clove garlic, crushed
6 cloves
1 teaspoon salt
1 teaspoon pepper
1 tablespoon sunflower oil

Cut 6 holes into the roast. In each hole stuff a few drops of vinegar, 1 pinch of crushed garlic, and 1 clove. Rub with salt and pepper. Set aside for 30 minutes. Preheat the oven to 350 degrees F.

Pour the oil in a shallow baking dish. Turn in the roast.

Bake for 40 minutes.

Serve hot with Eggplant Purée (page 93).

Roast Leg of Lamb

6 servings

2-pound leg of lamb
2 tablespoons salt
1 tablespoon pepper
4 cloves garlic, peeled
16 cloves
1 tablespoons allspice powder
2 tablespoons fresh thyme
1 tablespoon fresh rosemary
1 tablespoon sunflower oil
3 tablespoons chopped chives
3 tablespoons chopped parsley

Preheat oven to 350 degrees F.

Prepare the meat. Remove the skin and excess fat with a sharp knife. Rub with salt and pepper. Cut 8 slits into the roast with a sharp knife. In each indent, insert a 1/2 clove garlic, 2 cloves, and a pinch allspice powder. Turn in shallow oven dish greased with oil. Sprinkle with thyme and rosemary.

Cover the tip of the bone with aluminum foil. Roast for 45 minutes (20 to 25 minutes per pound). Sprinkle with chives and parsley.

Serve hot with red beans, Creole Rice (page 75), or a vegetable gratin.

Lentils and Bacon

6 servings

1 pound lentils
1/2 cup chopped Canadian bacon
1 teaspoon pepper
2 branches thyme
3 tablespoons chopped chives
2 tablespoons chopped parsley
1 red Scotch Bonnet pepper

In a large saucepan combine the lentils with 4 cups of water. Add the bacon, pepper, thyme, and chives. Bring to a boil and simmer over medium heat for 45 minutes.

Sprinkle with parsley.

Serve hot with red Scotch Bonnet pepper and Creole Rice (page 75).

Pork Colombo

6 servings

2-pounds pork loin, cut into pieces
2 tablespoons colombo powder
2 cups peeled and chopped onions
1 clove garlic, crushed
3 tablespoons freshly squeezed lime juice
2 teaspoons salt
1/2 teaspoon pepper
2 tablespoons oil
2 tablespoons fresh thyme
2 tablespoons chopped chives
3 tablespoons chopped parsley
1 teaspoon chopped Scotch Bonnet pepper
1 cup chopped eggplant
1 cup peeled and chopped green mango (optional)
1 beef bouillon cube

In a shallow dish, combine the meat with colombo powder, onions, garlic, 2 tablespoons of the lime juice, 1 teaspoon of the salt, and the pepper. Refrigerate for 3 to 4 hours.

In a large saucepan, heat the oil. Add the meat with marinade. Stir in the thyme, chives, parsley, Scotch Bonnet pepper, eggplant, and mango. Add the remaining 1 teaspoon of salt. Cover with water.

Cook over medium heat for 30 minutes. Add the bouillon cube and the remaining 1 tablespoon of lime juice. Stir well and simmer for another 5 minutes.

Serve hot with Creole Rice (page 75).

Roast Pork

6 servings

2 pounds roast pork taken from the loin
2 tablespoons freshly squeezed lime juice
3 cloves garlic, crushed
1 tablespoon salt
1 tablespoon pepper

Preheat oven to 350 degrees F.

Clean the pork under cold tap water. Rub it with lime juice. Cut slits in several places and stuff with the garlic cloves.

Season with salt and pepper. Turn into an oven dish and cook for 1 hour.

Serve hot with Eggplant Purée (page 93) or Stuffed Christophenes (page 109).

Sandra's Pork Stew

4 servings

1 clove garlic, crushed
1 cup peeled and sliced onion
2 tablespoons freshly squeezed lime juice
1 tablespoon salt
1/2 tablespoon pepper
2 pounds pork loin, cut into chunks
1/4 cup sunflower oil
2 tablespoons chopped chives
2 cloves

Combine garlic, onion, lime juice, salt, and pepper in a shallow dish. Stir in the pork and soak for 2 hours.

Heat the oil in a large saucepan. Brown the meat and seasonings for 10 to 15 minutes. Pour in 3/4 cup of water. Lower the heat and simmer 20 minutes.

Stir in the chives and cloves. Turn into a serving dish.

Serve hot with Creole Rice (page 75).

Coconut Chicken

6 servings

2 pounds chicken
1/4 cup sunflower oil
2 cups peeled and sliced onions
2 cups peeled and sliced carrots
2 clove garlic, crushed
1 cup dried white wine
2 cans (14 ounces each) coconut milk
1 tablespoon fresh thyme
1 bay leaf
1 tablespoon salt
1 tablespoon pepper

Cut the chicken into pieces. Combine the oil and chicken in a large saucepan. Cook over medium heat for 15 minutes until brown.

Stir in the onions, carrots, and garlic. Add the wine, coconut milk, thyme, and bay leaf. Season with salt and pepper.

Cover and simmer for 45 minutes over medium heat.

Serve hot with Creole Rice (page 75).

Chicken Colombo

6 servings

2 tablespoons sunflower oil
1 tablespoon butter
2 pounds chicken
4 tablespoons colombo powder
2 cups chicken broth
2 cups peeled and chopped onions
1 can (14 ounces) coconut milk
1 clove garlic, crushed
2 tablespoons freshly squeezed lime juice
2 tablespoons fresh thyme
2 tablespoons chopped chives
3 tablespoons chopped parsley
1 teaspoon chopped Scotch Bonnet pepper
1 tablespoon salt
1 tablespoon pepper
1 cup peeled and chopped bananas
1/2 cup shelled pistachios (optional)

In a large saucepan, heat the oil and butter. Stir in the chicken and colombo powder. Cook over medium heat for 15 minutes until brown.

Add the chicken broth, onions, 1/2 can of coconut milk, garlic, lime juice, thyme, chives, parsley, Scotch Bonnet pepper, salt, and pepper. Simmer over medium heat for 45 minutes. Turn off the heat.

Stir in the remaining 1/2 coconut milk, the bananas, and pistachios.

Serve hot with Creole Rice (page 75).

Mamie's Chicken with Mushrooms

4 servings

2 pounds free-range chicken, cut into pieces
2 limes, halved
2 tablespoons fresh thyme
2 tablespoons chopped parsley
1 onion, peeled and sliced
1/2 teaspoon pepper
1 teaspoon salt
3 tablespoons sunflower oil
2 cups sliced mushrooms

Place the chicken in shallow dish. Rub with lime and season with thyme, parsley, onion, pepper, and salt. Marinate for 30 minutes.

Heat the oil in a large saucepan. Stir in the chicken with seasonings. Brown over medium heat for 10 minutes. Stir in the mushrooms and cook for 5 minutes.

Lower the heat and cover with 1 cup of water. Stir well. Simmer for 25 minutes over low heat.

Serve hot with Creole Rice (page 75).

Lina's Chicken Fricassee

4 servings

1/4 cup freshly squeezed lime juice
1 clove garlic, crushed
3 tablespoons fresh thyme
5 tablespoons chopped chives
3 tablespoons chopped parsley
1 teaspoon chopped Scotch Bonnet pepper
1 clove
2 bay leaves
1 teaspoon Dijon mustard
2 pounds free-range chicken, cut into pieces
1/4 cup sunflower oil
1 cup peeled and chopped onion
1 lime, halved
1 clove garlic, peeled

The day before serving, prepare a marinade. In a shallow dish, combine the lime juice, crushed garlic, thyme, chives, parsley, Scotch Bonnet pepper, clove, bay leaves, and Dijon mustard. Add in the chicken. Cover and refrigerate overnight.

Preheat oven to 300 degrees F. Pour 1/2 cup of boiling water in the marinade. Stir well. Turn into a shallow oven dish. Roast for 30 to 40 minutes until brown. Baste regularly.

Remove the chicken and deglaze the marinade: pour in 1/2 cup of boiling water and stir well with a wooden spoon.

Heat the oil in a large saucepan. Add the chicken and onions. Brown for 5 minutes over medium heat. Stir in the marinade. Cover and simmer for 30 minutes.

Squeeze the lime over the chicken and add the peeled garlic clove. Stir well.

Serve hot with Creole Rice (page 75).

Daddy's Pineapple Ham

6 servings

2 pounds ham shoulder
4 cups brown sugar
2 cans (14 ounces each) sliced pineapple

Preheat the oven to 350 degrees F.

With a sharp knife, remove the fat from the ham shoulder and cut slits into the flesh. Coat the ham with 2 cups of the brown sugar. Bake in a shallow oven dish for 15 minutes.

Remove from the oven. Lower the heat to 250 degrees F.
Drain the pineapple slices and reserve the juice.

Prick the ham with cloves and coat with the pineapple juice and the remaining 2 cups of brown sugar. Arrange the pineapple slices around the ham.

Bake for 1 1/2 hours. Serve warm with bread and Parsley Butter (page 196).

Duck Flambé

4 servings

1 pound duck
2 tablespoons butter
1 tablespoon salt
1 tablespoon pepper
1 cup peeled and chopped onion
1 cup chicken broth
2 tablespoons white rum
2 tablespoons parsley

Cut the duck into pieces. In a large saucepan, melt the butter over medium heat. Add the duck, salt, and pepper. Cook for 10 minutes on each side. Stir in the onion and broth. Simmer over low heat for 40 minutes.

Heat the rum, pour over the duck and flambé. Sprinkle with parsley.

Serve hot with Creole Rice (page 75) or Plantain Gratin (page 102).

Turkey Wing Stew

4 servings

1 clove garlic, crushed
1 cup peeled and sliced onion
2 tablespoons freshly squeezed lime juice
1 tablespoon salt
1/2 tablespoon pepper
2 pounds turkey wings
1/4 cup sunflower oil
2 tablespoons chopped chives
2 cloves

Combine garlic, onion, lime juice, salt, and pepper in a shallow dish. Stir in the turkey wings and soak for 2 hours in refrigerator.

Heat the oil in a large saucepan. Brown the meat and seasonings for 10 to 15 minutes. Pour in 1/2 cup of water. Lower the heat and simmer 20 minutes.

Stir in the chives and cloves. Turn into a serving dish.

Serve hot with Creole Rice (page 75) and salted root vegetables.

Desserts

Being the eldest of a large number of siblings and cousins, I have attended many christenings and first communions. I remember looking forward to each of them. The traditional *Gâteau de Première Communion* dipped in the unctuous *Chaudau* prepared by my mother made each occasion worthwhile. In Martinique, this ceremonial dessert consists of *Pain Doux* or *Gâteau Fouetté* dipped in *chocolat* (hot cocoa).

During the Carnival festivities, when both young and old dress up for Vaval (the king of Carnival), my aunt Nicole prepared the lightest, most delicious fritters. My grandmother also prepares what I like to call *Crêpe Créole*, which are traditional French crêpes stuffed with lime and brown sugar. Another typical and popular dessert is the *Banane Flambée*, accompanied by an aged rum. Fruit tarts and pies are just divine. I recommend my aunt Codie's orange pie or the passion fruit pie. The guava sauce, my grandfather's creation, transforms any sorbet into a precious delicacy.

Jams are often eaten for dessert with fresh bread. It is an old custom adopted from the rural regions of France. Whether for breakfast or dessert, tropical fruit jams offer a distinct and bold taste as the flavor of the fruit comes out full force.

Desserts

Short Crust Pastry or Pâte Brisée

Flaky Pastry or Pâte Feuilletée

Aunt Serge's Sweet Potato Cake

Banana Flambée

Blanc-Manger

Chaudau de Maminette

Coconut Flan

Coconut Sorbet

Coconut Sugar Cakes

Cassava Crêpes

Crêpes Créole

Crystallized Papaya

Julie's Chocolate Cream

Gâteau Fouetté

Pineapple Jam

Prune Jam

Guava Jam

Guava Sauce

Guava Sorbet

Mont-Blanc

Nicole's Carnival Doughnuts

Orange Pie Tatie Codie

Passion Fruit Pie

Tourment d'Amour des Saintes

Short Crust Pastry or Pâte Brisée

Makes one 10-inch crust

1/2 cup butter, chilled
2 cups flour
1/2 teaspoon salt

Combine the butter, flour, and salt in a large bowl. Work with the fingers then quickly rotate the dough in the palms of the hands. Make a well and gradually pour in 5 to 6 teaspoons of water. Work until the dough becomes soft enough to gather into a ball. The dough should not be sticky to the fingers or the bowl. Cover and allow the dough to rest, refrigerated, from 2 to 6 hours.

Flaky Pastry or Pâte Feuilletée

Make one 10-inch crust

1 cup flour
1/2 cup butter, chilled
1/2 teaspoon salt
6 to 8 tablespoons ice water
1 egg yolk

Place the flour, butter, and salt in a food processor fitted with a steel blade. Pulse about 24 times, then open the machine and check the size of the crumbs. When the butter pieces are grain size, transfer the mixture to a large mixing bowl. Sprinkle 6 tablespoons of ice water onto the dough and mix. Squeeze a handful of the dough in your palm. The dough should have just enough moisture to stay together.

Line a 10-inch pie tin with the dough.

Preheat the oven to 375 degrees F. In a small bowl, combine the egg yolk with 2 tablespoons of water. Brush the rim of the pastry with egg wash.

Bake the pie shell for 15 minutes, then reduce the heat to 250 degrees F and continue to bake until it is an even golden brown, 8 to 12 minutes longer.

If the pie shell puffs up during baking, press down the center of the pastry with the back of a large spoon. Let cool.

Aunt Serge's Sweet Potato Cake

6 servings

2 pounds sweet potatoes, peeled and diced
3/4 cup bittersweet baking chocolate, melted
3/4 cup sugar
3/4 cup butter

In a large saucepan combine the sweet potatoes with 4 cups of water. Bring to a boil and simmer for 45 minutes. Drain and purée.

Preheat the oven to 350 degrees F.

In a large bowl mix the sweet potato puree with the chocolate, sugar, and butter. Stir well. Turn into a greased baking dish.
Bake for 30 minutes.

Serve cool.

Banana Flambée

4 servings

2 bananas
2 tablespoons butter
4 tablespoons sugar
1/2 cup white rum
1 lime, squeezed

Peel and halve the bananas lengthwise.

Melt the butter in a frying pan over medium heat. Brown the bananas 5 minutes on each side.

Add the sugar and pour in the rum. Cook for 2 minutes. Flambé.

Sprinkle with lime juice and serve at once.

Blanc-Manger

4 servings

8 sheets gelatine or 2 packets Knox unflavored gelatine
2 cups milk
3 cups grated coconut
1 1/2 cups whipping cream
3/4 cup brown sugar
6 coconut shells (optional)
1/2 cup shaved dark chocolate

Soak the gelatine sheets in 8 cups of cold water for 5 minutes. Drain. In using gelatine powder, dissolve in 2 cups of water until thick. Place a bowl in the freezer.

In a large saucepan bring the milk to a boil. Add 2 cups of the coconut and simmer for 5 minutes.

Stir in the gelatine. Simmer for another 10 minutes.

Drain the milk through a clean cloth above a large bowl. Let cool.

Combine the whipping cream and sugar in the chilled bowl. Beat until stiff. Delicately fold into the coconut milk. Turn into the coconut shells or other shallow dish. Refrigerate for 3 to 4 hours.

Sprinkle with the remaining 1 cup grated coconut and shaved chocolate before serving.

Chaudau de Maminette

8 servings

3 limes, grated (peels only)
2 tablespoons cinnamon
2 tablespoons almond extract
2 vanilla sticks
9 egg yolks
2 tablespoons cornstarch
4 cans (14 ounces each) sweetened condensed milk

In a large saucepan, bring 8 cups of water to a boil. Stir in 1/3 of the grated lime peel, the cinnamon, and almond extract.

Halve the vanilla sticks lengthwise. Grate the inside pulp over the saucepan, then add the sticks. Simmer over medium heat.

In a large bowl, beat the egg yolks with the remaining lime peels and cornstarch.

Add the condensed milk to the boiling water. Stir well and simmer. Set aside 1 cup of the hot milk in a bowl.

Quickly pour the cup of milk into the eggs and beat vigorously until smooth. Sieve. Then pour quickly into the saucepan containing the milk. Lower the heat. Stir constantly for 10 minutes until thick and creamy.

Serve warm with Gâteau Fouetté (page 174).

Coconut Flan

6 servings

1/2 cup brown sugar
1 3/4 cups coconut milk
1 cup milk
5 eggs, beaten
1/4 cup grated coconut
1 tablespoon cinnamon
1 tablespoon vanilla

In a shallow baking dish, combine 4 tablespoons of sugar with 2 tablespoons of water. Bring to a boil over high heat until caramelized. Remove from the heat and turn the baking dish around to spread evenly.

Preheat the oven to 200 degrees F. Combine the coconut milk, milk, and remaining 6 tablespoons sugar in a saucepan. Simmer over medium heat, stirring constantly until smooth.

Slowly stir in the beaten eggs, grated coconut, cinnamon, and vanilla. Pour into the shallow baking dish.

Place the baking dish into a large baking pan halfway filled with water. Bake in this double boiler for 2 hours. Let cool.

Refrigerate for 4 to 5 hours before serving. Remove from the baking dish.

Serve chilled.

Coconut Sorbet

6 servings

3 coconuts
4 cups brown sugar
2 tablespoons cinnamon
2 tablespoons nutmeg
2 tablespoons grated lime peel

Prepare the coconut milk. Break the coconut with a hammer. With a sharp knife detach the coconut flesh from the shell. Bring 2 cups of water to a boil. Grate the coconut flesh and pour over the boiling water. Soak for 1 hour. Drain the milk through a clean cloth above a large bowl.

Stir in the sugar, cinnamon, nutmeg, and lime peel. Let cool.

Stir into a sorbet machine for 40 minutes.

Serve with Guava Sauce (page 178).

Coconut Sugar Cakes

6 servings

2 coconuts
1 cup sugar
1 tablespoon cinnamon
1 vanilla stick
1 tablespoon lime peel
3 tablespoons food coloring

Break the coconuts with a hammer. Remove the flesh with a sharp knife and grate it.

In a saucepan combine the sugar, cinnamon, vanilla, and lime peel with 4 cups of water. Bring to a boil. Sieve. Add the grated coconut. Cook for another 25 minutes, stirring constantly.

When the mixture becomes thick remove from the stove. With a wooden spoon place small heaps of sugar cakes on a buttered tray.

Color the tops of the sugar cakes with food coloring. Let dry for 3 to 4 hours before serving.

Cassava Crêpes

6 servings

1 cup cassava meal
1 teaspoon double-acting baking powder
1/2 teaspoon salt
2 eggs
2 cups milk
1/4 cup sunflower oil
1/4 cup Nutella or chocolate fudge sauce

In a large bowl, combine cassava meal, baking powder, and salt. Make a well and add the eggs. Stir well. Add milk, stirring constantly until smooth.

Heat a 5-inch skillet. Grease it with few drops of oil. Add a small quantity of batter. Tip the skillet and let the batter spread over the bottom. Cook the crêpe over moderate heat. When brown underneath, turn it over and brown the other side. Use a few drop of oil for each crêpe.

Spread 1 tablespoon of Nutella on each crêpe. Roll or fold in half.

Serve warm.

Crêpes Creole

6 servings

1 cup flour
1 teaspoon double-acting baking powder
1/2 teaspoon salt
2 eggs
2 cups milk
1/4 cup sunflower oil
1 cup brown sugar
1/2 cup freshly squeezed lime juice

In a large bowl, combine flour, baking powder, and salt. Make a well and pour the eggs. Stir well. Add milk, stirring constantly until smooth.

Heat a 5-inch skillet. Grease it with few drops of oil. Add a small quantity of batter. Tip the skillet and let the batter spread over the bottom. Cook the crêpe over moderate heat. When brown underneath, turn it over and brown the other side. Use a few drops of oil for each crêpe.

Sprinkle each crêpe with 1 tablespoon of sugar and 1 teaspoon of lime juice. Roll or fold in half.

Serve warm.

Crystallized Papaya

6 servings

4 tablespoons freshly squeezed lime juice
6 cups peeled, seeded, and sliced ripe papaya
2 cups brown sugar
1 tablespoon olive oil

Combine 6 cups of water and lime juice in a large bowl. Add the papaya. Soak for 5 minutes. Drain.

In a large saucepan bring 6 cups of water to a boil. Poach the papaya for 5 minutes. Drain.

In a saucepan combine 4 cups of water with the brown sugar. Bring to a boil and simmer for 5 minutes until it turns into a thick syrup. Turn off the heat and add the papaya.

Once the syrup begins to harden, remove the papaya slices and place them on a tray greased with olive oil for 10 minutes. Sprinkle with sugar and let them cool off.

Serve at room temperature.

Julie's Chocolate Cream

4 servings

2 tablespoons flour
1/3 cup sugar
1 teaspoon cinnamon
1 teaspoon nutmeg
1 lime peel, grated
1 teaspoon almond extract
1 tablespoon cocoa powder
2 cups milk

In a medium saucepan combine the flour, sugar, cinnamon, nutmeg, lime peel, almond extract, and cocoa. Heat over low heat for 2 minutes. Add the milk and stir constantly for 15 minutes until thick and smooth.

Serve hot or cold.

Gâteau Fouetté

6 servings

6 eggs, separated
1 1/2 cups sugar
1 vanilla stick
1 lime peel, grated
1 1/2 cups flour

Beat the egg whites in a large bowl until firm. Stir in the egg yolks and sugar. Whip for 30 minutes.

Preheat the oven to 350 degrees F. Grease and flour a 4-inch deep and 8-inch wide cake pan.

Add the vanilla and lime peel to the eggs. Stir in the flour little by little until smooth. Turn into the cake pan. Bake for 45 minutes.

Serve warm with a Hot Cocoa (page 216) or Chaudau de Maminette (page 166).

Pineapple Jam

6 servings

2 pineapples
3 cups brown sugar
2 tablespoons cinnamon
2 tablespoons nutmeg

Remove the pineapple leaves. Peel with a sharp knife, removing all the black eyes. Halve, core, and dice.

In a saucepan combine the pineapple, 4 cups of water, the sugar, cinnamon, and nutmeg. Bring to a boil and simmer for 1 1/2 hours until the jam becomes very thick.

Turn into a jar and seal. Let stand overnight.

Prune Jam

6 servings

2 cups pitted prunes
2 cups brown sugar
2 tablespoons cinnamon
2 tablespoons nutmeg

In a saucepan combine the prunes, 4 cups of water, sugar, cinnamon, and nutmeg. Bring to a boil and simmer for 1 1/2 hours until the jam becomes thick.

Turn into a jar and seal. Let stand overnight.

Guava Jam

6 servings

2 pounds guava, peeled and diced
2 3/4 cups brown sugar
2 tablespoons cinnamon
1 tablespoon nutmeg
1 tablespoon grated lime peel

Puree the guava with 1/4 cup of water. Strain.

In a saucepan combine the guava purée, 4 cups of water, sugar, cinnamon, nutmeg, and lime peel.

Bring to a boil and simmer for 1 1/2 hours until the jam becomes creamy.

Turn into a jar and seal. Let stand overnight.

Guava Sauce

6 servings

2 pounds guava, peeled and diced
1 can (14 ounces) sweetened condensed milk
2 tablespoons cinnamon
2 tablespoons nutmeg
2 tablespoons grated lime peel

Puree and sieve the guava over a large bowl. Stir in the condensed milk, cinnamon, nutmeg, and lime peel. Add 2 cups of water. Stir well.

Serve with Coconut Sorbet (page 168).

Guava Sorbet

6 servings

2 pounds guava, peeled and diced
4 cups brown sugar
2 tablespoons cinnamon
2 tablespoons nutmeg
2 tablespoons grated lime peel

Puree and sieve the guava over a large bowl. Stir in the sugar, cinnamon, nutmeg, and lime peel.

Stir into a sorbet machine for 40 minutes.

Mont-Blanc

6 servings

For the Génoise:
1/4 cup butter, melted
6 eggs
1 cup sugar
1 teaspoon vanilla
1 cup flour

2 cans (14 ounces each) sweetened condensed milk
1 can (14 ounces) coconut milk
6 tablespoons cornstarch
3/4 cup brown sugar
1/4 cup dark rum
3 tablespoons shredded coconut

Preheat oven to 350 degrees F.

Prepare the génoise. In a double boiler, combine the eggs and sugar. Stir until lukewarm.

Beat 2/3 cup of the sugar and egg with a rotary or electric mixer for 8 minutes. Add the remaining 1/3 cup of mix. Increase speed and beat 2 minutes longer. Add vanilla, flour, and butter. Stir well.

Pour the batter into a greased and floured 6-inch deep and 10-inch round cake pan. Bake for 30 to 40 minutes. Turn out at once onto a plate. Let cool.

In a large saucepan, combine the condensed milk with coconut milk, cornstarch, and 3/4 cup of water. Bring to a boil over medium heat, stirring constantly.

Combine the sugar, rum, and 1 tablespoon of water in a bowl.

Cut the génoise into three disks. Place the bottom disk on a serving dish. Spread 1/3 of the rum and 1/3 of the coconut cream. Place the second disk over and repeat. Close with the third disk and cover the cake with the remaining rum and cream.

Sprinkle with grated coconut.

Nicole's Carnival Doughnuts

6 servings

1/3 cup butter
1/2 teaspoon brown sugar
1/2 cup flour
4 eggs
1 teaspoon almond extract
1 teaspoon cinnamon
1 teaspoon vanilla extract
4 cups sunflower oil
3/4 teaspoon powdered sugar

Melt the butter in a large saucepan over low heat. Stir in the sugar. Bring to a boil and turn off the heat. Pour the flour all at once. Stir vigorously with a wooden spoon until smooth. Heat over medium heat and stir until elastic and smooth. Turn off the heat. Add the eggs one by one stirring constantly. Add the almond, cinnamon, and vanilla.

In a large saucepan heat the oil. Drop in 4 teaspoons of dough and brown. Once cooked on one side the doughnut will roll over by itself. Drain on a colander lined with paper towels. Repeat with the rest of the dough.

Sprinkle with powdered sugar. Serve warm.

Orange Pie
Tatie Codie

6 servings

Short Crust Pastry (page 161)
1/3 cup butter
5 egg yolks
1/2 cup brown sugar
1/2 cup freshly squeezed orange juice
2 teaspoons grated lime peel

Preheat the oven to 350 degrees F. Roll the dough into a circle and line a 9-inch pie pan. Prick with a fork in several places. Bake the crust for 15 minutes. Let cool.

Melt the butter in a double boiler over medium heat. Stir in the egg yolks, sugar, orange juice, and lime peel. Stir for 5 to 8 minutes until thick and creamy. Turn into the pie pan. Bake for 20 minutes.

Serve warm.

Passion Fruit Pie

6 servings

Short Crust Pastry (page 161)
5 passion fruits, halved
1/3 cup butter
5 egg yolks
1/2 cup brown sugar
2 teaspoons grated lime peel

Preheat the oven to 350 degrees F. Roll the dough into a circle and line a 9-inch pie pan. Prick with a fork in several places. Bake the crust for 15 minutes. Let cool.

Purée the pulp of the passion fruits in a blender. Sieve until obtaining a clear syrup.

Melt the butter in a double boiler over medium heat. Stir in the egg yolks, sugar, passion fruit syrup, and lime peel. Stir until thick and creamy. Turn into the pie pan. Bake for 20 minutes.

Serve warm.

Tourment d'Amour des Saintes

4 servings

Short Crust Pastry (page 161)
1 cup coconut (guava or banana) jam
3 eggs
1/2 cup brown sugar
1/4 cup flour
1 grated lime peel
1 teaspoon vanilla

Preheat the oven to 350 degrees F.

Line a 10-inch pie tin (or four 3-inch individual pie pans) with the short crust. Prick with a fork. Spread the coconut jam over the crust.

Combine the eggs, sugar, flour, lime peel, and vanilla. Pour onto the coconut jam.

Bake for 25 minutes. Cover with aluminum foil. Bake for another 10 minutes.

Serve warm.

Sauces, Spreads, and Bread

The recipe for *Sauce Chien* is a well-kept family secret. Just like tomato sauce in Italy, each family has its own and it is the best! This spicy sauce can accompany any grilled fish and shellfish. Its taste brings out the flavor of the meat. I inherited my father's *Sauce Chien* and over the years, I added my own twist to it.

The hot peppers in the French Caribbean are from the Scotch Bonnet pepper family. They add a delicious taste to any meal—the trick being to use them in adequate quantities. They are very strong and it is advisable to replace them with Stuffed Scotch Bonnet pepper confit oil. A few drops suffice to flavor a whole dish.

Lastly, one of the most carefully and lovingly prepared foods in French Caribbean cuisine is definitely the bread. The French baguette found in Guadeloupe and Martinique compares to the Parisian one. All the French pastries including *croissant*, *pain au chocolat*, and *pain au raisin* are locally made. My favorite are the *Pains Nattés* or small braided bread when they just come out of the oven. Another local bread is the *Danquit*. Sold by street vendors around the markets, it makes a delicious snack when paired with a fresh passion fruit juice.

Sauces, Spreads, and Bread

Béchamel Sauce

Béchamel Sauce with Eggs

Béchamel Sauce with Onions

Sauce Chien

Spicy Mayonnaise

Parsley Butter

Uncle Ary's Fish Butter

Scotch Bonnet Pepper Confit

Danquits

Dombrés

Béchamel Sauce

4 servings

3 tablespoons butter
6 tablespoons flour
2 cups milk
1 tablespoon chopped chives
1/4 teaspoon nutmeg
1/2 teaspoon salt
1/4 teaspoon pepper

Melt the butter in a saucepan over low heat. Add the flour and stir until smooth and creamy.

Slowly pour in the milk, stirring constantly until thick. Add the chives, nutmeg, salt, and pepper. Simmer over low heat stirring constantly for 15 minutes until thick and creamy.

Béchamel Sauce with Eggs

4 servings

3 tablespoons butter
6 tablespoons flour
2 cups milk
2 egg yolks, beaten
1 tablespoon chopped chives
1/4 teaspoon nutmeg
1/2 teaspoon salt
1/4 teaspoon pepper

Melt the butter in a saucepan over low heat. Add the flour and stir until smooth and creamy.

Slowly pour in the milk, stirring constantly until thick. Stir in the egg yolks.

Add the chives, nutmeg, salt, and pepper. Simmer over low heat, stirring constantly for 10 minutes until thick and creamy.

Béchamel Sauce with Onions

4 servings

3 tablespoons butter
1 cup peeled and sliced onions
6 tablespoons flour
2 cups milk
2 egg yolks, beaten
1/2 teaspoon salt
1/4 teaspoon pepper

Melt the butter in a saucepan over low heat. Brown the onions over low heat for 10 minutes. Add in the flour and stir until smooth and creamy.

Slowly pour in the milk, stirring constantly until thick. Stir in the egg yolks.

Season with salt and pepper. Simmer over low heat, stirring constantly for 15 minutes until thick and creamy.

Sauce Chien

4 servings

1/4 cup chopped chives
1/4 cup peeled and chopped onion
2 cloves garlic, crushed
2 tablespoons chopped parsley
1 teaspoon chopped Scotch Bonnet pepper
3 limes, squeezed
2 tablespoons sunflower oil
1 teaspoon salt
1 teaspoon pepper

Bring 2 cups of water to a boil.

In a bowl combine the chives, onion, garlic, parsley, and Scotch Bonnet pepper. Stir in the lime juice, oil, salt, and pepper.

Pour the boiling water over the onion mixture and infuse for 5 to 10 minutes.

Serve with grilled fish and Creole Rice (page 75).

Spicy Mayonnaise

6 servings

1 egg yolk
1 teaspoon Dijon mustard
1/2 teaspoon salt
1/2 teaspoon pepper
1 cup oil
1/4 teaspoon cayenne pepper
1 lime, squeezed

In a bowl combine the egg yolk, mustard, salt, and pepper. Stir well with a wooden spoon.

Drizzle in 1/4 cup of oil stirring constantly until all the oil is absorbed. Repeat with the rest of the oil until obtaining a thick mayonnaise.

Add the Cayenne pepper and lime juice. Stir well.

Serve with grilled lobster or fish.

Parsley Butter

6 servings

2 cups butter
4 tablespoons finely chopped parsley
4 tablespoons chopped chives
1 clove garlic, crushed
2 teaspoons salt
2 teaspoons pepper
1 teaspoon chopped Scotch Bonnet pepper

Set the butter at room temperature for 2 to 4 hours.

In a large bowl, combine the butter with parsley, chives, and garlic. Season with salt, pepper, and Scotch Bonnet pepper. Knead well.

Turn in a 4 by 5-inch pan. Refrigerate overnight.

Serve with bread and Daddy's Pineapple Ham (page 153).

Uncle Ary's Fish Butter

4 servings

1/4 cup chopped parsley
3 tablespoons fresh thyme
4 tablespoons chopped chives
1/2 teaspoon salt
1/2 teaspoon pepper
1 1/4 cups cleaned white fish
1/ 2 cup chopped smoked fish
1 cup butter, melted
4 tablespoons olive oil
2 egg yolks
1 clove garlic, crushed
1/4 teaspoon cinnamon
1/4 teaspoon nutmeg
1/3 teaspoon seeded and chopped Scotch Bonnet pepper

In a large saucepan combine the parsley, thyme, chives, salt, pepper, and fresh fish. Add 6 cups of water. Bring to a boil and simmer for 25 minutes. Drain. Bone and skin the fish.

Crumble the flesh over a large bowl. Stir in the smoked fish. Add the butter, olive oil, egg yolks, garlic, cinnamon, nutmeg, and Scotch Bonnet pepper. Stir well with a fork until smooth.

Turn into a blender and purée. Pour into a bowl and refrigerate overnight.

Replaces plain butter in all dishes.

Scotch Bonnet Pepper Confit

3/4 pound red Scotch Bonnet pepper
1/4 cup calcite salt
1 cup sunflower oil

The red peppers are extremely hot and it is better to execute the recipe with latex gloves on.

Remove the Scotch Bonnet peppers tails and chop with a fork and sharp knife.

Lay the salt at the bottom of a jar. Fill with half of the Scotch Bonnet peppers. Sprinkle 1 tablespoon of salt. Add the rest of Scotch Bonnet peppers and salt. Pour in the oil and close tightly. Refrigerate for 3 days.

You will obtain a very flavored and hot oil. Only a few drops of oil or a piece of Scotch Bonnet pepper are necessary to flavor a dish.

Danquits

4 servings

1 cup flour
4 teaspoons butter, melted
1/2 teaspoon baking powder
1 teaspoon salt
1/2 cup oil

Combine the flour, butter, baking powder, and salt in large bowl. Add 1/2 cup of water and knead well. Add flour if necessary. The dough should be smooth and elastic. Form a ball and let rest for 1 hour.

Flour your hands and roll the dough into 3-inches ball. Flatten each ball into 1-inch thick circles.

Heat the oil in a frying pan and fry the danquits 4 minutes on each side until golden. Drain with paper towels.

Serve warm with red beans or a salad. Also used to make delicious sandwiches.

Dombrés

6 servings

1 cup flour
1 1/2 tablespoons salt

Combine the flour, salt, and 1/4 cup of water. Knead well until smooth and elastic. Add flour if necessary. Roll into a ball and let rest for 1 hour.

Prepare the dombrés. Flour you hands and roll the dough into 2-inch balls.

Bring 4 cups of water to a boil. Add the dombrés and poach for 10 to 15 minutes.

Usually, the dombrés are added to soups at the end of cooking time. Serve hot.

$\mathscr{D}$rinks

Surprisingly, French Caribbean drinks are mostly served in small glasses with one ice cube. Of course, one will find elaborate cocktails in hotels and resorts, but typically consumed drinks are much more straightforward. The local fishermen are known to start the day with a glass of straight rum called *décollage* (take-off) while playing dominos.

The most popular drink in Guadeloupe and Martinique is the *Ti Punch*. It is made with sugar cane syrup, lime, and rum, and each of these ingredients can be adjusted to taste. The quality of the rum varies from a plantation to the other. The rum *Bologne* made in Guadeloupe is my personal favorite. Because of its exquisite taste, *Ti Punch* has started to appear in bars and restaurants. Lately, I have found *Ti Punch* listed on the menu of several bars in New York City.

The *Schrubb* is the traditional drink of Christmas celebrations. Macerated for years with orange peel, sugar, and spices, the rum takes on a bold and festive flavor. There is almost a punch for every fruit that grows in the islands. All of them are made more or less by seeping the rum with fruits, sugar, and spices for several months.

Drinks

Sugar Cane Syrup

Banana Punch

Coconut Punch

Pineapple Punch

Planteur

Schrubb

Star Fruit Juice

Ti-John's Limeade

Ti Punch

Hot Cocoa

Sugar Cane Syrup

6 servings

1 cup brown sugar
1 vanilla bean, halved

Combine the sugar with 1 1/2 cups of water in a medium jar. Stir until sugar dissolves. Add the vanilla bean.

Sugar cane syrup can also be bought in specialty stores. It can replace regular brown sugar in many drinks, such as the popular Ti Punch.

Banana Punch

4 servings

5 cups peeled and diced ripe bananas
1/4 cup freshly squeezed lime juice
3/4 cup sugar cane syrup (page 205)
1/2 cup crème fraîche
1 cup white rum

Purée the bananas with lime juice in a blender. Add the sugar cane syrup, crème fraîche, and rum. Mix well until smooth.

Serve chilled with ice cubes.

Coconut Punch

4 servings

2 cups white rum
2 cans (14 ounces each) coconut milk
1/4 cup Sugar Cane Syrup (page 207)
1 teaspoon cinnamon
1 teaspoon nutmeg
1 vanilla bean, halved
1 lime peel, grated

In a blender mix the white rum, coconut milk, sugar cane syrup, cinnamon, nutmeg, vanilla bean, and lime peel. Turn into a glass bottle. Macerate for 2 days.

Pour 1/4 cup of coconut punch in 4 small glasses. Add one ice cube in each glass.

Pineapple Punch

4 servings

4 cups peeled and diced pineapple
1/4 cup brown sugar
2 cups white rum

Puree the pineapple flesh in a blender. Stir in the brown sugar. Mix well. Turn into a saucepan and bring to a boil for 20 minutes. Let cool.

Cover with white rum. Turn into a tall jar. Stir well. Refrigerate for 2 hours.

Serve chilled in small glasses.

Planteur

8 servings

2 cups freshly squeezed orange juice
1 cup aged dark rum
1 cup Sugar Cane Syrup (page 207)
1 tablespoon angostura bitters

Combine the orange juice, rum, sugar cane, and angostura bitters in a large bowl. Stir well. Transfer into a glass bottle, close and shake.

Macerate for 2 weeks.

Pour about 1/4 cup in 8 small glasses. Serve with ice cubes.

Schrubb

6 servings

2 orange peels
4 cups white rum
2 cups Sugar Cane Syrup (page 207)
1 cup seeded and diced prunes
1 vanilla bean, halved
2 tablespoons cinnamon
1 teaspoon whole coffee beans

Cut the orange peels into 2-inch strips. Combine with the rum in a jar. Macerate for 4 days.

Remove the orange peels. Add the sugar cane syrup, prunes, vanilla, and cinnamon. Macerate for 3 days.

Sieve. Add the coffee beans and turn into a glass bottle.

Serve at room temperature. The Schrubb is traditionally served at Christmas.

Star Fruit Juice

4 servings

4 pounds star fruits, sliced
1 cup brown sugar
1/4 cup freshly squeezed lime juice

Purée the fruits in a blender. Filter through a sieve. Add 2 cups of water.

Stir in sugar and lime juice.

Serve chilled.

Ti-John's Limeade

6 servings

1/2 cup freshly squeezed lime juice
1/4 cup freshly squeezed orange juice
1/2 cup brown sugar
6 teaspoons grated lime peel

Combine the lime and orange juice with sugar and 6 cups of water.

Stir and serve chilled sprinkled with grated lime peels.

Ti Punch

4 servings

4 tablespoons Sugar Cane Syrup (page 207)
4 lime wedges
1 cup white rum
4 ice cubes

Drop 1 tablespoon of syrup each into 4 glasses. Add a lime wedge, 1/4 cup of rum, and 1 ice cube to each glass. Stir well.

The Ti Punch is served with Codfish (page 35) or Vegetable (page 46) Fritters (Accras).

Hot Cocoa

6 servings

5 cups milk
1 vanilla bean, halved lengthwise
1/3 cup cocoa powder
1 tablespoon cinnamon
1/2 cup brown sugar
1/2 teaspoon almond extract
2 tablespoons cornstarch

Bring 4 cups of milk to a boil in a large saucepan. Stir in the vanilla bean. Add the cocoa powder, cinnamon, sugar, and almond extract. Simmer over low heat for 5 minutes.

In a small bowl combine the remaining cup of milk with the cornstarch. Slowly turn into the cocoa.

Stir constantly for 5 minutes.

Serve hot.

Bernard Lamotte/© Vogue, Condé Nast Publications Inc.

Shopping Places

Most of the products included in French Caribbean cooking can be found in regular supermarkets and grocery stores. Because French Caribbean cuisine is multicultural, it is a good idea to check Indian, Middle Eastern, or Asian markets and groceries for exotic fruits, vegetables, spices, and fish.

Here is a list of websites where specific ingredients such as cassava meal or colombo powder can be purchased.

Websites:

www.afrifood.com Caribbean imported foods that include plantains, tropical fruit, beverages, spicy jerky, and frozen vegetables.

www.beachbohio.com Products of the Caribbean and Puerto Rico.

www.boutique-creole.com Great gift baskets with Creole spices, pepper sauces, jam, and cassava meal.

www.caribbeandelights.com Imported Caribbean sauces, seasonings, coffees, gift baskets, and cookbooks.

www.carib.freeservers.com Caribbean and South American gourmet food and drink products including coffee, jams, cassava biscuits, spices, jerk seasonings, and pepper sauces.

www.caribimports.com Online shopping for Caribbean hot sauces, condiments, spices, tropical fruit products, jerk, and fiery food lovers' products. Most products are also available wholesale.

www.creoleshop.com Great resource for colombo powder and other French Caribbean delicacies.

www.cubanfoodmarket.com Cuban food specialties delivered anywhere. Same day shipping: bread, coffee, desserts, cookbooks, and art.

www.galaxymall.com/virtual/things-caribbean
Trinidadian, Jamaican, Guyanese, and Caribbean food products and ingredients.

www.howjax.com Caribbean-style chutneys and condiments. Has vegetarian or hot and spicy flavors with menu list.

www.icatmall.com/peppahouse Caribbean hot sauces in tropical fruit flavors, sold individually or in gift packs.

www.native-treasures.com Caribbean-style sauces and seasonings. Has recipes, newsletter, and shopping form online.

www.PRProducts.com Tropical candy from Puerto Rico and Mr. Luma cigars from the Dominican Republic.

www.rummi.com Caribbean-style jellies, cakes, coffee, fish, and sauces. Includes recipe and product catalog.

www.trinifood.com Includes grocery items such as canned vegetables, fruits, jams, condiments, and beverages direct from the Caribbean Islands. Online shopping form and prices provided.

Index

D

E

F

G

H

J

L

M

O

P

R

S

T

V

Also by Stéphanie Ovide

COOKING IN THE FRENCH FASHION
Recipes in French and English
Stéphanie Ovide
Illustrated by Maurita Magner
FRANCE IS RENOWNED for its contributions to worlds of cuisine and fashion, and this cookbook captures the essence of both!

Featuring 38 bilingual recipes, *Cooking in the French Fashion* offers unique insight into the art of contemporary French cuisine. Popular recipes—both traditional and contemporary—are all adapted for the modern North American kitchen. Sample such stylish delicacies *Blanquette de veau* (Veal Blanquette), *Artichauts vinaigrette* (Artichokes with Vinaigrette Sauce), *Gigot d'agneau aux flageolets* (Leg of Lamb with Flageolets) and *Mousse au chocolat* (Chocolate Mousse) among many others.

With the illustrator's enchanting fashion sketches throughout, *Cooking in the French Fashion* is the perfect gift for any cook, novice or gourmand, who wants to learn more about the French palate, culture and language.
93 PAGES • 5 X 7 • 0-7818-0739-5 • $11.95HC • (139)

CREOLE (CARIBBEAN)-ENGLISH/
ENGLISH-CREOLE (CARIBBEAN) DICTIONARY
Stéphanie Ovide
THIS DICTIONARY FEATURES THE COMMON VOCABULARY used in Haiti, St. Thomas, Guadeloupe, Martinique, Dominica, St. Lucia, Grenada, Trinidad, French Guyana, and Louisiana. It is a very useful companion for anyone traveling to the Caribbean who would like to communicate directly with the inhabitants. Because much of the charm and exoticism of the islands are also in the language, one cannot fully understand the Caribbean culture without apprehending the Creole language.

Common-sense pronunciation and a section on Creole proverbs complement this indispensable travel companion.
8,000 ENTRIES • 268 PAGES • 4 X 6 • 0-7818-0455-8 • $11.95PB • (351)

Other Hippocrene French Titles

FRENCH-ENGLISH DICTIONARY OF GASTRONOMIC TERMS
Bernard Luce
20,000 ENTRIES • 500 PAGES • 5 1/2 X 8 1/2 • 0-7818-0555-4 • $24.95PB • (655)

FRENCH-ENGLISH/ENGLISH-FRENCH
DICTIONARY & PHRASEBOOK
5,500 ENTRIES • 233 PAGES • 3 3/4 X 7 1/2 • 0-7818-0856-1 • $11.95PB • (128)

BEGINNER'S FRENCH

Marie-Rose Carré

465 PAGES • 5 1/2 x 8 1/2 • 0-7818-0863-4 • $14.95PB • (264)

FRENCH-ENGLISH/ENGLISH-FRENCH PRACTICAL DICTIONARY

Rosalind Williams

35,000 ENTRIES • 5 1/2 x 8 1/2 • 0-7818-0178-8 • $9.95PB • (199)

HIPPOCRENE CHILDREN'S ILLUSTRATED FRENCH DICTIONARY

"HERE COMES A COMPLETELY NEW ENGLISH-FRENCH DICTIONARY for small children, ages 5-10. With 500 words illustrated in beautiful colors and with nice pictures, this dictionary covers all aspects of everyday life: animals, flowers, games ..."—*Journal Français*

- for ages 5 and up
- 500 entries with color pictures
- commonsense pronunciation for each French word
- French-English index

500 ENTRIES • 94 PAGES • 8 1/2 x 11 • 0-7818-0710-7 • $14.95HC • (797)
500 ENTRIES • 94 PAGES • 8 1/2 x 11 • 0-7818-0847-2 • $11.95PB • (663)

FRANCE: AN ILLUSTRATED HISTORY

Lisa Neal

214 PAGES • 5 x 7 • 50 B/W ILLUS./MAPS • 0-7818-0872-3 • $12.95PB • (340)

PARIS: AN ILLUSTRATED HISTORY

Elaine Mokhtefi

150 PAGES • 5 x 7• 50 B/W ILLUS./MAPS • 0-7818-0838-3 • $12.95PB • (136)

TREASURY OF FRENCH LOVE POEMS, QUOTATIONS AND PROVERBS

Edited and translated by Richard A. Branyon

THIS BEAUTIFUL GIFT VOLUME contains poems, quotations and proverbs in French with side-by-side English translation. Includes elections from Baudelaire, Hugo, Rimbaud and others. Also available in audio cassette read by native French speakers and American actors.

128 PAGES • 5 x 7 • 0-7818-0307-1 • $11.95HC • (344)
AUDIOBOOK: 0-7818-0359-4 • $12.95 • (580)

TREASURY OF CLASSIC FRENCH LOVE SHORT STORIES IN FRENCH AND ENGLISH

Edited by Lisa Neal

These 10 short stories span eight centuries of French literature. Nine celebrated French writers are represented: Marie de France, Marguerite de Navarre, Madame de Lafayette, Guy de Maupassant, Rétif de la Bretonne, Alphonse Daudet, Auguste de Villiers de

l'Isle, Gabrielle-Sidonie Colette, and Jean Giono. The text includes the original French with side by side English translation.
159 PAGES • 5 X 7 • 0-7818-0511-2 • W • $11.95HC • (621)

DICTIONARY OF 1,000 FRENCH PROVERBS

Edited by Peter Mertvago

Organized alphabetically by key words, this bilingual reference book is a guide to and information source for a key element of French.
131 PAGES • 5 X 8 • 0-7818-0400-0 • $11.95PB • (146)

COMPREHENSIVE BILINGUAL DICTIONARY OF FRENCH PROVERBS

Monique Brezin-Rossignol

FRANCIS BACON ONCE REMARKED THAT THE GENIUS, wit and spirit of a nation can be discovered in its proverbs. This unique bilingual collection includes 6,000 French proverbs, arranged in alphabetical order in French and English.
6,000 ENTRIES • 400 PAGES • 5 X 8 • 0-7818-0594-5 • $24.95PB • (700)

Other Hippocrene Cookbooks From the Americas

A TASTE OF HAITI

Mirta Yurnet-Thomas & The Thomas Family

WITH AFRICAN, FRENCH, ARABIC AND AMERINDIAN INFLUENCES, the food and culture of Haiti are fascinating subjects to explore. From the days of slavery to present times, traditional Haitian cuisine has relied upon staples like root vegetables, pork, fish, and flavor enhancers like *Pikliz* (picklese, or hot pepper vinegar) and *Zepis* (ground spices). This cookbook presents more than 100 traditional Haitian recipes, which are complemented by information on Haiti's history, holidays and celebrations, necessary food staples, and cooking methods. Recipe titles are presented in English, Creole, and French.
180 PAGES • 5 1/2 X 8 1/2 • 0-7818-0927-4 • $24.95HC • (8)

CAJUN WOMEN COOK: RECIPES & STORIES FROM SOUTH LOUISIANA KITCHENS

Nicole Fontenot & Alicia Fontenot Vidrine

IN THIS TREASURY OF CAJUN HERITAGE, the authors allow the people who are the very foundations of Cajun culture to tell their own stories. They visited Cajun women in their homes and kitchens and gathered over 300 recipes as well as thousands of narrative accounts. Most of these women were raised on small farms and remember times when everything (except coffee, sugar, and flour) was homemade. They shared traditional recipes made with modern and simple ingredients.
330 PAGES • 6 X 9 • 0-7818-0932-0 • $24.95HC • (75)

A TASTE OF QUEBEC, SECOND EDITION

Julian Armstrong

FIRST PUBLISHED IN 1990, *A Taste of Quebec* is the definitive guide to traditional and modern cooking in this distinctive region of Canada. Now revised and updated, this edition features over 125 new recipes and traditional favorites, along with highlights on up-and-coming new chefs, the province's best restaurants, notes of architectural and historical interest, and typical regional menus for a genuine Quebecois feast. With photos illustrating the people, the cuisine, and the land sprinkled throughout, this is *the* food lover's guide to Quebec.

200 PAGES • 8-PAGE COLOR INSERT • 7 3/4 x 9 3/8 • 0-7818-0902-9 • $16.95PB • (32)

ARGENTINA COOKS!

Shirley Lomax Brooks

ARGENTINE CUISINE IS ONE OF THE WORLD'S best-kept culinary secrets. The country's expansive landscape includes tropical jungles, vast grasslands with sheep and cattle, alpine lakes and glacier-studded mountains. As a result, a great variety of foods are available—game, lamb, an incredible assortment of fish and seafood, exotic fruits and prime quality beef. This cookbook highlights recipes from Argentina's nine regions, including signature recipes from Five Star chefs, along with the best of collections from the author and other talented home chefs.

298 PAGES • 6 x 9 • 0-7818-0829-4 • $24.95HC • (85)

CUISINES OF PORTUGUESE ENCOUNTERS

Cherie Hamilton

THIS FASCINATING COLLECTION OF 225 AUTHENTIC RECIPES is the first cookbook to encompass the entire Portuguese-speaking world and explain how Portugal and its former colonies influenced each other's culinary traditions. Included are dishes containing Asian, South American, African, and European spices, along with varied ingredients like piripiri pepper, coconut milk, cilantro, manioc root, bananas, dried fish, seafood and meats. The recipes range from appetizers like "Pastel com o Diabo Dentro" (Pastry with the Devil Inside from Cape Verde), to main courses such as "Frango à Africana" (Grilled Chicken African Style from Mozambique) and "Cuscuz de Camarão" (Shrimp Couscous from Brazil), to desserts like "Pudim de Côco" (Coconut Pudding from Timor). Menus for religious holidays and festive occasions, a glossary, a section on mail-order sources, a brief history of the cuisines, and a bilingual index will assist the home chef in creating meals that celebrate the rich, diverse, and delicious culinary legacy of this old empire.

378 PAGES • 6 x 9 • DRAWINGS • 0-7818-0831-6 • $24.95HC • (91)

ART OF SOUTH AMERICAN COOKERY

Myra Waldo

THIS COOKBOOK OFFERS DELICIOUS RECIPES for the various courses of a typical South American meal, with specialties from all countries. Dishes show the expected influence of Spanish and Portuguese cuisines, but are enhanced by the use of locally available ingredients.

272 PAGES • 5 x 8 1/2 • 0-7818-0485-X • $11.95PB • (423)

ART OF BRAZILIAN COOKERY
Dolores Botafogo
IN THE 40 YEARS SINCE its original publication, *The Art of Brazilian Cookery* has been a trusted source for home chefs through the decades. This authentic cookbook of Brazilian food, the first of its kind to be published in the U.S., includes over 300 savory and varied recipes and begins with a vivid historical-geographic and culinary picture of Brazil.
240 PAGES • 5 1/2 x 8 1/4 • 0-7818-0130-3 • $11.95PB • (250)

OLD HAVANA COOKBOOK
Cuban Recipes in Spanish and English
CUBAN CUISINE, THOUGH DERIVED FROM ITS MOTHER COUNTRY, Spain, has been modified and refined by locally available foods like pork, rice, corn, beans and sugar, and the requirements of a tropical climate. Fine Gulf Stream fish, crabs and lobsters, and an almost infinite variety of vegetables and luscious, tropical fruits also have their places on the traditional Cuban table. This cookbook includes over 50 recipes, each in Spanish with side-by-side English translation—all of them classic Cuban fare and old Havana specialties adapted for the North American kitchen. Among the recipes included are: Ajiaco (famous Cuban Stew), Boiled Pargo with Avocado Sauce, Lobster Havanaise, Tamal en Cazuela (Soft Tamal), Quimbombó (okra), Picadillo, Roast Suckling Pig, and Boniatillo (Sweet Potato Dulce), along with a whole chapter on famous Cuban cocktails and beverages.
123 PAGES • 5 x 7 • LINE DRAWINGS • 0-7818-0767-0 • $11.95HC • (590)

MAYAN COOKING: RECIPES FROM THE SUN KINGDOMS OF MEXICO
Cherry Hamman
TAKE A CULINARY JOURNEY into the Mexican Yucatan, to unravel the mysteries of the ancient Mayan diet! This book contains over 150 traditional recipes that date back several centuries, as well as contemporary creations that represent Maya ingenuity and imagination in borrowing new foods and ideas.
275 PAGES • 6 x 9 • DRAWINGS • 0-7818-0580-5 • $24.95HC • (680)

Prices subject to change without prior notice. TO PURCHASE HIPPOCRENE BOOKS contact your local bookstore, call (718) 454-2366, or write to: HIPPOCRENE BOOKS, 171 Madison Avenue, New York, NY 10016. Please enclose check or money order, adding $5.00 shipping (UPS) for the first book, and $.50 for each additional book.